The Unexpected Guest

A Surprising Journey

Jan Guest

The Uninvited Guest: A Surprising Journey

Copyright @2003 by Jan Guest
All rights reserved.

Living Legacy Press
603 Louis Henna Boulevard, S B-107 #122
Round Rock, Texas 78664

Editor-in-Chief — Mindy F. Reed, The Authors' Asistant

Book Design and Printing — Morgan Printing

Cataloging-in Publication Data

Guest, Jan
The Uninvited Guest: A Surprising Journey

    p.   cm.   photos

1. Memoir—self-actualization. 2. Guest, Jan—memoir 3. Family life—United States
I. Title II. Author III. Biography IV. Monograph

ISBN 0-9729552-2-4

HV   818.54 GU

Printed in the United States of America

DEDICATION

To
Eloise Montgomery Guest and Roy Oberly Guest
who gave me life.

To
Paul, Melissa and Lorri
who completed my life.

To
Elisabeth, Austin, Jamie and Montanna
who continue my life

Acknowledgements

I have heard many writers say, "This book would not have happened if it were not for...." This is also true in my case. If it were not for Mindy Reed, I would not have finished this book. She encouraged me when I did not think I could go on, inspired me when I felt hopeless, held my hand when I was in despair and walked me through the whole process with good cheer and humor. Mindy I love you.

I want to acknowledge my parents. They loved me in spite of their chaos. And I love them.

My children have been the focus of my life. I love them beyond words. I thank them for teaching *me* so many valuable lessons, and my grand-daughters whom I adore, continue the lessons.

To my "dream group," you know who you are. Thank you for your love and support. And to Helen, Ginnie, and Kyoko, who let me read and cry and encouraged me to do more. I love you all.

An especial thanks to Katya Walter who assisted greatly in my becoming the woman I want to be. I love you Katya.

Y mi vida, FAF, te amo.

Author's Note

This is my story. This is *my* perception of some of the events in my life. If there are those who remember it differently, then that is *their* story. The people and places I write about are written with love and respect. And I hope some humor. The names have been changed out of respect.

Everything can be taken from a man but one thing: the least of the human freedoms—to choose one's attitude in any given set of circumstances, to choose one's own way.

— Viktor Frankl
Man's Search for Meaning

1

A Time to be Born,
A Time to Die

I was born in a two-room house, the home of my aunt and uncle. My parents were visiting, or perhaps living with them again. It was difficult times for them: again. My entry into the world was at an unexpected time. I arrived in the middle of August, out in the country, miles from anywhere. And hot! Hotter than Hell. No air circulated, flies circled around like buzzards in a deathly silence except, I imagine, for my mother's screaming.

I was her fourth baby in five years, which included two boys, Roy and Jack, and a girl, Voncile, who died at birth. Then there was me. Or trying with all my might to be me, whoever that was. All I wanted was to be born, to be held, and to be loved and revered.

Aunt Sealy caught me, cleaned me up and whispered in my ear, "Love all people, no matter they's color. We alls' the same."

We were in the middle of the *Great Depression*, deep in poverty where jobs were so scarce they didn't really exist. Deep in the South where my twenty-three-year-old mother and thirty-three-year-old father were faced with yet another mouth to feed.

Aunt Sealy was the midwife. I first saw her when I was six years old. I remember seeing and being so afraid of the black woman. She was not much larger than I was at six, and was all hunched over. She reminded me of a gnarled, knobby, weathered-worn tree trunk. She always walked with a cane that seemed taller than she was, and it was every bit as gnarled. She had no teeth and seemed to be very impatient with children, dog, or anything that got in her way. I always wondered why she birthed us babies if she didn't like us as we got older.

Nonetheless, Aunt Sealy brought a bunch of us into this world. I was six years old when she died and I went to her funeral. That funeral was an impressionable moment on my young history, one to this day, I will never forget. Aunt Sealy, herself, had many children, the exact number changed depending on whom you talked to, but it was more than thirteen, and they were all at her funeral. The funeral was held at a little country church. My Aunt Myrtle (Daddy's sister), whom we were living with at the time, dressed me, and my cousin, (who really wasn't my cousin) in our Sunday-go-to-meetin' clothes. We walked to the church, which was probably a mile down the road, but seemed longer to my six-year-old legs.

The heat in South Georgia is notorious. The steam rising off the dirt roads makes you feel like you're in a plastic trash bag with no air holes. The air clings to your skin and feels like an extra set of clothes. We walked in that heat to the church.

At the church, where *we* sat in the back, women and men fanned themselves with palmetto fans. However, it was not the rhythmic fanning that caught my attention; it was the crying, screaming and moaning as members of Aunt Sealy's community went to view her in the casket. One of her daughters tried to climb into the casket with her. This really upset me because I didn't understand where Aunt Sealy was going or why her daughter would want to go with her. Aunt Sealy's casket was braced on two chairs. The front of the church was covered with flowers, mostly from Aunt Sealy's and Aunt Myrtle's yards. People were falling over each other to get to the casket, and others, like her daughter, tried to climb in. I clung to Aunt Myrtle's dress and put my fingers in my mouth as we approached the casket. I knew Daddy didn't like me sucking on my fingers, but I didn't know what else to do to feel safe. After the service they buried Aunt Sealy in the small graveyard beside the church. Little did I know that Aunt Sealy's funeral would be one of many in the next several years of my life.

2

Childhood Memories

The family was always busy with their own things. Daddy reading the newspaper, mother ironing or mending, Jack and Roy playing and me, at two-years-old, left to entertain myself. I wanted attention, but everybody else was occupied. I tried to get anyone to pay attention to me, but everyone was too busy and no one wanted to be bothered with a two-year-old girl. So I did the only thing that brought me attention. I got on the rung of daddy's rocking chair and said, "*Daddy, I row my sew in fire, Daddy, I row my sew in fire.*"

I said this about five times before someone screeched, "Daddy, Jan's new shoes are burning up in the fireplace!" That got me everybody's attention then. More than I wanted and in places I wouldn't have suspected. I soon learned that getting attention was not positive.

———— •———

My first memory of my brothers, Roy and Jack, was them telling me that they didn't like me or want me in the family because I wouldn't eat turnip greens, corn bread, onions or drink ice tea. Their complaints made it obvious that there was something wrong with me. I don't think they were right, because to this day I love turnip greens, corn bread, onions and ice tea. Maybe it was just a case of developing a digestive system worthy of such sumptuous food.

———•———

I think I was about three the first time I knew something was not right in our household. We were living out in the country at least two miles away from any neighbors. Daddy was not at home, but Mamma was making the bed and I was helping her. I must have done something wrong because the next thing I knew a large bar of soap was whizzing past my head. It was fortunate that bar of soap missed my head, otherwise, I would not be here writing this today. I was little and that bar of soap weighed at least a pound. It was lye soap, a hard, heavy weapon. My mother was mad! But what had I done to create such a fury? I didn't know and there were many times when I would wonder what had I done to have these things going on around me? How was I to blame? I was told that I was dumb, stupid and ugly. If I were just smarter, more clever, prettier, then everything would be okay. Everybody in my family would be calm, happy, content and together. But that was not the case and would never be the case. My immediate family, which included Mamma, Daddy, Roy, my oldest brother by almost six years, and Jack, the younger brother who was three years my senior. There was a girl born between Jack and me, but she was born dead. How did my mother cope with that? I never heard. It was never discussed. My mother had four children in less than six years. No wonder she was angry. She was tired, worn-out and under appreciated.

We learn how to please and to fit into our environment. We also learned not to trust. How could we trust anyone when we were told one thing, then saw the opposite acted out, then very quickly told something totally different? We didn't know what the truth was, but we were instructed on how our family was to believe and to act. *Don't tell the neighbors, no one is to know what we are doing behind closed doors.* It was very confusing.

15

There was a time, maybe when I was a still a toddler, that Daddy brought this woman in to live in our house. To this day I can not understand how my mother could put up with that. In my little child's mind I didn't have anything against that woman, she was nice to me, but I knew in the belly of my being that what was going on in that house was not right. Mamma was pretty upset and there was a lot of screaming and yelling going around. Finally Mamma set the woman's suitcases out on the porch and told Daddy, "Get her out of here and I mean now!" My parents continued to live together, fight, leave, get back together again, and repeat the cycle over and over again.

However, I can remember a few good times that we had when I felt that we really did have a family. But that was not often. It was mostly conflict, confusion and running to keep Daddy from beating up on Mamma. Also saving souls on Sunday, that is after we had raced around the city to be safe from him on Saturday night.

Daddy was a large man, six feet tall, but he was not fat. He had brown/black hair and brown eyes. In his later years he wore glasses that gave his eyes a penetrating look, which was scary at times. It seemed like his eyes could pierce right into your guts and tell if you were lying or not. Or whatever mischief he thought you might be in. I escaped most of that rage, although I don't know how that happened. However, my oldest brother Roy received all that I didn't get and more. It seemed that whenever Daddy was in a rage, it was Roy or Mamma who caught the brunt of it. Mamma caught it often; most of the time Daddy would go after Roy, then Mamma would get in between them to keep Roy from getting killed, and it was Mamma who ended up with black eyes, bruised arms, chest, legs, and wherever else Daddy hit her. How we could exist as a family one way and appear to outsiders another way?

It was a mystery to me. I did not know this story until I was well into my adulthood. I was home visiting Mamma, and her friend Leasy told me about seeing us walking downtown when we first moved to Moultrie. She said she was working in a dress shop and was looking out the window since not much business was going on. She saw this beautiful family walking past her window, down the sidewalk. She walked closer to the door to get a better look and admire the beauty and elegance of that family. I was curious to know whom she was talking about. I had been gone from Moultrie for a long time, but I thought that I might remember this family. She told me it was Mamma, Daddy and me. I nearly fell over. She said we were walking down the street with me in the middle, holding both my parents' hands, and we all looked so happy. She said she envied us our happiness, our family, our togetherness. She later became a good friend of Mamma's, and we learned through the years that she was a battered wife, who almost died once and was hospitalized several times. And she envied us!

Little did she know that when we returned home or later that night or sometime soon, her friend Eloise would be bolting for parts unknown in order to escape Reverend Roy. Yes, I said *Reverend Roy*, Roy Oberly Guest was a minister in the Southern Baptist Church. He was a very charismatic man and could hold an audience in the palm of his hand. They came far and wide to hear my daddy speak. Yet, he was also a wife beater and an occasional binge drinker.

As I said, I do remember that there were good times when we seemed to have a happy family, although those moments didn't last long. We would start out on an upbeat note, everybody talking, laughing, usually eating, then out of the blue, Daddy would go into a rage. I could never figure out what caused these pure, unmitigated rages from hell. Not a clue.

The fun times, short as they were, did exist. For example, there was the time Roy brought home Tiny. Tiny was a little bit of fluff, black hair, smaller than a drowned rat. Roy had her in a one pound sugar sack, with room to spare. Daddy and Mamma took one look at her and told him we couldn't keep her. After about five minutes of the most ungodly caterwauling you have ever heard, they gave in. When I started bawling it was bad enough but when Jack and Roy joined me it was bedlam. Daddy took Tiny out onto our back porch, along with a pair of tweezers and a small bottle of ink. We had no idea what was going to happen, but since we were told we could keep her we didn't figure him to kill her. So as quiet as we could be, we watched Daddy as he put Tiny up on the table, talked to her in a low, sweet voice, then he started rubbing her fur. Tiny just kinda lay there, probably not knowing if she was going to meet her Maker or what was going to happen. Daddy took the tweezers and started pulling off ticks, fleas, and other vermin that had decided to live on Tiny. He sat there, as patient as I had ever seen him, and methodically pulled out every living thing that had inhabited Tiny. It took a considerable amount of time, but he never appeared tired or yelled, or got impatient. He joked with Mamma, kidded around with Roy, and showed us how the ink killed the ticks. After he finished, he washed Tiny with Ivory soap and asked, real politely, for us to get him a towel. Jack, Roy, and I tried to outrun each other to find a towel to give to our fantastic, doctoring father. He had performed a miracle and we knew it. Tiny was not long for this world when Roy bought her home, and none of us thought she would live through the night. We knew she was of hardy stock being part Spits and part German Shepherd. She was small in size, but her stance was pure German Shepherd. Her ears stood up straight as a soldier, and she was jet black with a couple of tiny white hairs at her neck. We thought she could smile, and Jack and I told our Aunt Mary, who told everyone she knew that Tiny could sit on the potty. We almost killed her by feeding her handfuls of caramels.

She would jump on the couch where she wasn't suppose to sit, and we would pretend that Mamma was coming and holler out, "Here comes Mamma," then she would jump down, and shyly look around to show our mother that she wasn't on the couch. No dog was ever loved more than Tiny and she loved us back, unconditionally. She gave us seven years of pure joy, love and loyalty.

When we left on a trip or to go to town, Tiny was left outside. When we returned, as the car moved up the driveway, she would circle the car, running around and around the car, head pitched to the heavens, emitting a yaooooooooooooooo. She continued to do this until we got out of the car, hugged her, played with her and brought her inside with us. We loved her as only one can love an animal, with all our hearts.

One day, we had been out for the afternoon and didn't think much about Tiny not meeting us when we drove up. Later one of us asked where Tiny was and we all realized we had not seen her since we we had gotten home. There had been some pretty heinous happenings up and down our street and we all suspected one neighbor of poisoning our pet, but I couldn't comprehend how anyone, not even evil, old Mrs. Johnson could poison our

Tiny. Such innocence. We found Tiny up under Mrs. Cook's house, poisoned. Our hearts were pierced and the tears unselfconsciously flowed. I don't remember Roy ever crying (he always said he was too tough to cry), but he was wailing away with the rest of us. I never got over Tiny. To this day, I have not had a pet because I could not let my unrestrained love flow like that again. I have stayed aloof. I also felt that way about men for a long time.

——•——

I am told that I was enterprising from the time I was about four. Daddy took me into the town of Graham and while we were there I saw a red rocking chair, just my size. I asked the man how much it was and he told me a dollar. I said, "That's too much, I'll pay fifty cents." I didn't know that Daddy was standing behind me nodding his head at whatever I said. That was the prettiest red chair I had ever seen, and if he had held his price I'm sure I would have paid it since money, which I didn't have, meant nothing to me.

How could the same man who could save a puppy's life, buy his daughter a red rocking chair, be caring with his sons, be the same man who could humiliate his wife, embarrass his children and God only knows do what to himself?

I remember when I was living with my aunt and uncle. We called her Aunty (pronounced Ahntee); I didn't know her real name. I didn't understand why my parents were not there or when they were coming back. One Sunday, which was no different than other Sunday afternoons in South Georgia, humid, hot with the blowflies zooming in and out of the house, Aunty and Son, Aunty's husband, were entertaining their minister and his wife. They had all been to church in the tiny, country community where Aunty and Son lived. Aunty made fried chicken, mashed potatoes, gravy, along with tomatoes picked from the garden out back and a big gallon of ice tea. The minister and his wife spent the afternoon there with their baby girl, who was just at the age to crawl. As she played, everyone sat trying to keep cool with hand fans from the funeral home.

I don't know where we had been, if anywhere, I just know that we arrived at my aunt's house on a hot Sunday afternoon. I know they had company and we were intruding. But we did that often, intrude. Mamma and Daddy left me, age seven; my brother Roy, age thirteen; and my brother Jack, age ten, at my aunt's house. I fell on the bed, crying, wailing and heartbroken. My mamma was gone, my daddy was gone and I didn't know, again, what I had done wrong. They left us without a reason, without a backward glance. I don't know what my brothers did or felt. I was too consumed with my own grief, desolation and bewilderment. Why? Why did they leave? Why couldn't I go with them? Why? Why? Why?

My cousin Peggy came into the room where I lay on the bed, crying, and said, "Jan, let's play with the baby. The baby is so cute and we can play with her."

I shook my head, put my fingers in my mouth and cried.

Peggy and I were crazy about babies. Once Aunty told us that the neighbor, who lived a mile over, was going to have a baby and that we should stand on the porch and watch out for the stork. She said when we saw the stork, to come and tell her because the stork would have the baby and we could go and see it. All afternoon until it was dark and we could no longer see the sky from where we stood on the porch. The next day we looked but we were told the neighbor had a little girl. Again, the stork had fooled us.

Peggy really wasn't my cousin, but we were told that we were cousins and that was good enough for me. Except that everyone knew Peggy was not Aunty and Son's baby girl. Son had a brother who had thirteen children; Peggy was the last one. When Peggy was born, Son's sister-in-law died, so Son and Aunty took the baby as theirs. Peggy was over eighteen years old when she learned that she had twelve brothers and sisters. Aunty had threatened the life of anyone who told Peggy the truth. I was a believer that Aunty would carry out her threat. This is the same woman who chased thirteen-year-old Roy a mile down the country lane, a butcher knife in her hand, hollering all the way, "You little heathen, eating my sausage I had out for supper tonight." The same woman who, when we were in the woods picking wild violets, had a hoe over her shoulder, said, "Stop children, don't move." She swung that hoe over her head and connected with the head of the rattlesnake, who would never again scare little children to death. I never told Peggy she was not Aunty and Son's child.

Peggy and I learned how to say fuck together, which I knew meant we were going to hell. We were sitting on the porch one day, nothing to do so we started rhyming truck, buck, luck, duck and without knowing what the word meant said, "fuck." We both covered out mouths, scared a bolt of lighting was going to smite us and send us to hell. We ran away from each other and never in our lives acknowledged that we had said that word. I have used it a few times since, but she probably hasn't. Like my friend said, "We never used that word unless we were doing it, did we?"

When we were teenagers I told her not to get married but to have a career and get out of Graham. She didn't listen to me, got married at eighteen, had two daughters and lived within a five-mile radius of the old homestead. But I never told her she wasn't Aunty and Son's child.

My brothers and I stayed with Aunty for a year. I was in second grade and we had to ride the bus to school. There was only one school for all grades, and several grades were in one room. We also had outdoor toilets, which got to be interesting because it was a one-seater for all those children. Aunty also had an outdoor toilet that I hated. It was smelly and there was never enough Sears-Roebuck catalog; just corncobs and cornhusks to wipe yourself. I would hold it and hold it until finally forced to go. I think I ruined my colon.

Mamma came to visit occasionally, and sometimes she would pick me up from school. I don't know where she was living, just that it wasn't with us. When she picked me up, I got so excited I put my fingers in my mouth. I was painfully shy and terribly self-conscious because I knew it was not right for us to be living with my aunt and uncle when they didn't have money enough to feed themselves let alone three more hungry mouths. That's what I heard "Three more hungry mouths to feed."

There were a lot of women who came over to pick up my daddy. He wasn't at my Aunty's often, but when he was he would only be there a short time, then go off with some woman. I guess he just came there to sleep. Mrs. Smith was a woman who picked up Daddy and she was a puzzle to me. She had three children of her own, but they were in an orphanage. I wasn't sure what an orphanage was, but I knew I didn't want to go to one. One day she came to get my daddy and she was in a big, black, shiny car. I didn't know about cars, but I knew this was a big, fancy one. Aunty and Son never had a car.

There were a lot of ladies around; some picked him up in their cars, and some sat on Aunty's back porch with him and played the guitar and sang to him. I hated them and I knew that was another reason why I was going to hell, because I wasn't supposed to hate.

Aunty's place was just a two-room house. Not a two-bedroom house, but a house with two rooms. While we were there, Son's daddy lived with them; three nephews of Son's were also there. That made ten of us in a two-room house. The kitchen was attached and that was where we ate and Aunty cooked for all of us, itinerant field hands and any hobos that came by. She would get up before any of us and fire up the cook stove. She'd go out and chop fire wood; cook breakfast; feed all of us; cleaned the dishes and the kitchen; make-up the bedding; get us dressed, and then go out to work in the fields, chopping cotton or whatever else needed doing. She worked until lunch time (or dinner as the country people called the middle of the day meal), then go cook and start the process all over again while the men ate, then napped on the front porch before they went back to the fields. Aunty would go back to the fields, working till suppertime. Many times we would all be in bed, and she would be working by lamplight, mending clothes, preparing ingredients for the next day's meal or whatever. I know she died from being worn out. With all those people depending on her, she never took care of herself and died at age fifty-five of uterine cancer.

I wanted to be like Aunty. Not the hardworking Aunty, but the Aunty who could stand on the back porch, spread her legs and pee, standing up. The pee never ran down her legs and on to her feet like it did mine when I tried it. I aspired to be able to pee without seeing the pee cascading down my leg onto my dust-covered feet, making little hieroglyphics. She also dipped snuff, and when Peggy and I were six we wanted snuff. Aunty could sit on the porch and zero in on one of the chickens pecking at worms in the yard and hit him bullseye! I wanted to spit like Aunty. To pee and to spit were my biggest ambitions.

Aunty mixed cocoa and sugar and put it in a snuff tin and gave it to Peggy and me. We went around all that day dipping, putting the mixture into our bottom lip and talking like we were tongue-tied. It was such ecstasy.

Mornings were very intense at Aunty's. We would get up, dress, eat our biscuit and then wait for Peggy. Peggy would not eat a single meal unless she had a saucer of syrup. When the maple syrup ran out. Aunty would mix coffee and sugar, and Peggy would dip her biscuit in it. Peggy didn't like to go to school and that caused a lot of consternation. I loved school and was always eager to go until Peggy started crying and hiding behind the door and making Aunty drag her to the school bus. Aunty would almost be in tears from the struggle, so a lot of days we wouldn't go to school. I was disappointed when we didn't go to school, but Peggy, Jack and I would play school instead. Peggy was always the teacher and she would rap out knuckles with a peach twig since we didn't have a ruler.

When we did go to school we would ride the bus, forever it seemed. The bus picked up other white children. We would get to school, me running to my classroom, Jack and Roy lagging behind, and Peggy almost at a standstill. I would no sooner get in my class than Roy would come knocking at the door to tell the teacher he wanted his little sister Janis. I would leave the classroom, and there outside were Jack and Peggy waiting for me. We were going home. We lived a couple of miles from the school so we would start walking down that dusty, white sandy road. We'd finally get home and Aunty would get us some fresh water from the well. I don't ever remember us getting scolded or in trouble for leaving school because if Peggy wanted to leave, it was Roy's responsibility to gather us together and get us back to Aunty's house. Roy, thirteen, was the oldest and he looked out for us. He beat up every boy and a couple of girls who rode on our bus. At school he beat up the town boys. He was a very angry kid, and I guess all the beatings he took from our father said to him that he was to beat up everybody he could. Daddy told all of us that if we got into trouble with a kid and didn't beat him to a pulp that Daddy would beat us to a pulp when we got home. Roy took that threat as seriously as I did when Aunty said that she would kill anyone who told Peggy she wasn't Aunty and Son's child.

One morning we got on the bus. In the next house over, about a mile from Aunty, lived the Johnson family. They had a bunch of kids of all ages and sizes; some of them went to school with us and rode the same bus. One of the Johnson boys was about Roy's age and told Roy that morning that his older sister had married our daddy the weekend before. Roy beat that boy to a pulp. We knew that woman had been around our daddy a bunch of times, but we didn't think that it could be true, that he had married her because he was still married to our mother. Or so we thought, but we hadn't seen them for a long time so we didn't know for sure. Roy beat-up that boy just in case.

Aunty and Son had a Victrola and when Son would have a little too much moonshine on Saturday nights, he would play records and dance with us, or with Aunty. On those nights he was a loving, gregarious man, but the rest of the time he was a quiet, unassuming man. On Saturday night he would play the pump organ and sing and I loved those times the most. He would play *You Are My Sunshine*, *Smile, Smile, Smile*, my favorite, and act as if he were on Major Bowes' radio show. Peggy and I would put our heads behind the radio, a big wooden cabinet, and sing like we were on the Grand Ole' Opry. Seldom were batteries available to put in the radio, so we made our own music.

Grandpa was old. He was Son's father, but everybody called him Grandpa. He would holler at us kids, telling us to quiet down, and he gave each of us a name. Mine was Spinning Jenny and Peggy's was Cricket. Any child who came to visit left with a new name from Grandpa. He was funny and I think we laughed at him at his expense.

Aunty would stand at the lone fireplace, in the front room. That was the room where Roy, Jack, Son, Grandpa and the three older boys slept. Aunty, Peggy, Jack and I slept in the back room. Aunty would stand at the fireplace putting on cold cream and Grandpa would ask for some, not being able to see, and she would tell him it was some kind of jam. How we would laugh when Grandpa would spit all over the place from the acrid cold cream.

We didn't have lamps at night because kerosene was too expensive to burn. As soon as supper was over the lampshades were removed and washed, and the wicks trimmed for early the next day.

Aunty had one more talent that I aspired to, which was that she could stand at the fireplace and fart into the next county, throw her head back

24

and laugh the most delicious, joyful laugh I had ever heard. How I loved it when she farted even as choking as it might be, just so I could hear that infectious laugh.

In the summertime Aunty would have a dinner in the backyard. Folks from the community gathered planks and put them on sawhorses to make tables. Everybody in the county and beyond would come, bringing covered dishes with the most delicious food that's ever been prepared. There were platters of Southern fried chicken; fresh from the garden sliced tomatoes; potato salad made with green bell pepper; fried okra; corn on the cob; turnip greens; biscuits and my aunt's special lemon cake made just for me. Lots of watermelon, peaches, cantaloupes and other fruits were served. We would feast, as the little kids ran all over the place and older people sat in the lawn chairs, fanning themselves with fans from the funeral home. The younger people went around to the other side of the house to smooch. Lots of activity and lots of fun took place, and for a moment times were happy.

———•———

It was late at night; Jack and I were on pallets on the floor, and Peggy and Aunty were in the bed. There was a quiet that only exists in the country. So quiet you could hear the tiniest noise. I was not asleep, a little drowsy, but as usual having difficulty getting to sleep. Years later my husband would say it was like I was standing guard over the world until daylight came. Mostly I was waiting to see if I had to get up and run from the beatings.

Aunty got up from her bed, shook me and said, "Janis, get up and come with me." I started to ask why but she shushed me, "Don't wake up Peggy." I got up not knowing what we were going to do. It was so cold. I always hated getting up in that cold, when the fire in the fireplace was not burning very big; it was freezing. I followed her out the door to the back porch. The moon was big, shining on the backyard like a muted floodlight. Aunty lifted up her arm and I saw she had a gun in her hand. She hollered, "Get out of my hen house, I'll shoot your head off," I was shaking now from fear, the cold forgotten. Aunty fired off a shot, the sound bounced off the barn, the outhouse and jumped into the next county. I heard flap, flap, flap, as feet hit the ground and someone was running.

As he jumped over the fence I heard a small voice say, "yessum, Miss Myrtle, I ís gone," and more flap, flap, as he ran down the road.

"Okay, Janis, go back to bed and go to sleep now, you hear?"

"Yessum," I said as I shook all the way back to bed. It was curious to me, there were two grown men, three young men approaching eighteen (who later went into World War II) and my two brothers, along with another girl who was a year older than I was. Yet she got me up to chase the chicken thief out of the hen house.

While we were at Aunty and Son's my other aunt would send us boxes of clothes. Aunt Mary was the truant officer of Palm Beach County, Florida and she collected clothes for needy children and there were none needier than her brother's. Aunty would go through the clothes, picking, sorting, putting the frilly, pretty clothes in one pile for Peggy and then seeing if there was anything left over that, "Janis could wear." What clothes didn't come from Aunt Mary, Aunty made from flour sacks. A few times we got to go to town. Graham had a population of about 250 people, two stores, a post office, a Shell service station and five churches. We would study those flour sacks with such intensity, visualizing dresses made from this one or that one, picking out our favorites. Aunty would make us a dress after all the flour was gone. She would also fix our hair, making us "pretty as pictures." Only her vexation with my hair would bring out words she didn't use around us very often. She would cut strips from brown paper bags and roll our hair around those strips till we had little knots all over our head. Peggy had blond (some of the neighbors said Aunty bleached it, which she vehemently denied, but I knew she put lemon juice in the rinse water) hair and ringlets like Shirley Temple. Aunty refused to take her on a train or out of town for fear that she would be stolen right out from under her because, "Peggy is so incredibly beautiful." Peggy didn't have the trouble I had with hair. My hair was bone straight, fine, limp and wouldn't hold a curl even if Aunty threatened it with her gun, hoe or butcher knife. The brown paper bag strips would stay in my hair all night; knots all over, my head hurting. I begged Aunty to please let me take them out, "No," she would say, "your hair will curl if you will be patient." I'm still waiting.

Three times a week the rolling store would come. That was great excitement. We might, if Aunty could find an egg or two, get a piece of bubble gum. Aunty would take one piece of bubble gum, cut it in four pieces and give a piece to Jack, Roy, Peggy, and me. I know my piece lasted me till the next time I got one, which would be two or three days till those blessed chickens would lay again. The smells of candy, rat-trap cheese, pickles in the barrel and tobacco all mixed and mingled in the air. It was enough to send a small child to food heaven. I craved everything I saw. Aunty bought a bottle of Durkee's Dressing and I had never had any before. I drank the whole bottle, puked all night and have never had any since. The same thing was true with chocolate covered cherries.

On those late nights when everyone was asleep and I could hear Son and Grandpa snoring, I would hear the ripple of paper, softly being torn. So quiet, it was a silent tearing and I knew that Aunty had bought a piece of chocolate candy just for Peggy. She would hide it until she thought everyone was asleep and then she would give it to Peggy. Didn't she remember I was the child who stood guard over her hen house, awake all night to make sure we were all protected? She meant well.

———•———

The most excitement occurred during tobacco season. In the spring the tender young shoots were planted. Then the mule pulled a cart while a field hand sat at the back of the cart and put down the shoots. Another hand walked behind with a large vat of water, watering the plants. Another came behind the water boy and closed up the holes. The tobacco was nursed through droughts, torrential rains and winds that could top off the shoots leaving them impotent. It was a whirlwind existence for the tobacco and the tobacco growers. The big barn down from the house was repaired and made ready to do the curing when the tobacco was ready. Frequently at night, during curing season, we would see a huge orange glow in the distance, and all the farmers would hurry to their neighbor's house, knowing that the tobacco barn was on fire. Someone would sit all night in the barn, watching the curing fire, keeping the heat at a degree positive for curing. Lots of jibes were given when someone was suspected of falling asleep while watching the fire and tending the curing. When the tobacco was picked from the fields, it was brought up to the barn where several families would go together to string the tobacco and get it ready for curing. When that family finished, it was on to the next farm, and everybody would congregate there to get the tobacco ready for that farmer. That was a lot of fun because there were always people around, lots of babies to be played with and put to sleep. Mothers and wives cooking, cooking, cooking to feed all those hands. When the tobacco was finished curing, they would take a sheet full and put it on the front porch and we would sit there culling the tobacco. One pile for grade A, another pile for a lesser grade and a pile for the farmers. Then it was off to the town and to the tobacco warehouses to sell. Oh, the smell was divine. I have never smoked; I tried several times, but it made me sick. Still the smell has always held a very masculine aura for me. In the fall we would have the same type of activities, only this was for gathering sugar cane and grinding it into syrup. The horses would go round and round, grinding the cane and we would play and sip cane juice.

Most things that were not too pleasant seemed to happen at night. Anytime a car came down the lane Peggy could identify who it was and what kind of car. I never learned to do that and couldn't figure how she could distinguish the different sounds of cars. They all sounded alike to me. But one night she didn't know whose car it was, even as it was turning into the yard in front of Aunty's house. It was my mother, father, and a man and woman whom I had never seen before. I was pretty sure Daddy was drinking because he smelled funny and he was acting all lovely-dovey, joking with Roy, hugging on Mamma, "acting the fool," as Aunty would say.

We were all packed up and in the car before I knew what was happening. The man was driving, Roy was in the middle beside the strange woman. The woman kept leaning into Roy and telling the man she had a new boyfriend. I didn't think that was right, but I was just a little kid. I don't know how Roy felt because that woman kept kissing on him and pulling him up next to her. Jack sat in the back with daddy in the middle, mom on the side and me in her lap. Something else I didn't like and didn't think it was right, at least with me there. Daddy kept pulling on Mamma and putting his hand up her dress and pushing me aside. I didn't like that, and Mamma kept saying, "Stop, Obie, stop it" and Daddy would laugh. What I was really afraid of was that Daddy would get mad and start a fight.

3

Daughter of a Preacher Man

I was eight when we moved to Jacksonville, Florida, and into an apartment. Housing was very difficult to get during those days of World War II. Daddy had been in the army in the first war, and now that World War II had started he had enlisted in the marines.

We lived in an upstairs apartment. It was a big, white, wood house. We lived next to an ice cream store similar to a Dairy Queen. One day I was standing on the sidewalk, and a woman and a little girl passed by me. Both the woman and the little girl were licking ice cream cones. The woman turned around and said, "Here, take this coupon and go get you an ice cream cone." I didn't say anything. I was too shy. But another emotion came over me that I would experience over the next several years. I was ashamed. I didn't know why. It was a nice gesture that the woman made, but I guess I had heard too many times, "another mouth to feed," and felt she just looked at me and knew that I was needy. I didn't get that ice cream cone and I didn't tell anyone about it. We usually got into trouble for telling what other people said to us. I learned not to tell.

Once at the dinner table, everything was going nicely, everyone was peaceful, enjoying the good food that was on the table. I listened to Daddy who was telling us about his honorable discharge from the marines because of his foot. He had somehow broken a small bone in his foot, and it caused lots of pain especially when he would go on maneuvers. I told him that the people downstairs had asked me if he had a discharge and I had said "yes." He began to yell at me, "did you tell them I had a honorable or dishonorable discharge?" I got all confused with the two words. I couldn't remember if I said honorable or dishonorable. He blew a gasket and we were in trouble for days after that. I began to pay attention to words from then on. However, I have always had test anxiety; I question myself unrelentingly, "Do I have the right word or not?"

The good times in Jacksonville were when Daddy would buy a big bunch of shrimp and Mamma would cook them up. We would have a feast and a good time. Mother would cover the kitchen table with old newspapers and put a box of saltine crackers, a bottle of catsup and the bowl of shrimp in the middle of the table; each of us would have a big Coca-Cola in the big green bottles. We would sit around the table and eat, laugh and be a family.

One of the things that I had to do that caused me shame was obeying Daddy's order to go to the little store down from our house and get him beer. Asians ran the store and they would pour beer into Chinese carry-out containers. Daddy would order me to hurry, but if I ran, half-ran, or walked fast I would slosh the beer and it would spill. But if I cautiously and patiently walked, keeping the beer level and not sloshing I would get fussed at for not getting there fast enough. I always felt guilty when I would look at the storeowner, not sure what he was thinking but knowing in my child's heart no little girl should be buying beer.

World War II was on and we had rules to comply with, such as we could not have lights on after dark and we had to keep our window shades drawn. There had to be a strip of black tape over the top part of the car's headlights. Gas was rationed, so we couldn't use the car very often. Food was rationed. Daddy and I would go to my school where we took our coupons and get our ration of sugar, oleo and gas. The oleo margarine was white, a lard like substance, with a yellow packet of coloring which we would mix with the lard like stuff to make "butter;" margarine actually. When Mamma got the margarine and sugar, she would make us a sweet treat.

On mornings after loud, raucous, frightening, screaming fights the woman in the apartment below us would have my mother and me to come down for tea. I thought that was so elegant, tea. She put little lacy place mats on the table, teacups with saucers, and long, tapered, cinnamon sticks to put in our tea. She also had some kind of cookies that I had never seen before. I thought she was very elegant and from a world that I didn't know. We drank our tea, and she talked to me as if I were an adult. My shyness would dissolve and I could talk to her. I wondered if she knew what went on in our household upstairs, but I never talked to her about that, especially after the debacle over the words honorable or dishonorable.

One night there was a lot of yelling and fighting. I finally became exhausted from the tension and drifted into a light sleep. I was suddenly shaken awake by my mother's admonishments, "shush; hurry; be quiet; get dressed. "Get up, get dressed, don't make any noise," she cautioned me.

"What is it?" I whispered back to her.

"We've got to run, hurry now," she told me. I didn't need to know more than that. I hurriedly got dressed and we were out of the house, running, silently breathing, fleeing the enemy. Fleeing my dad. Soon he would be on a prowl, yelling at Mamma, screaming about anything and nothing, at least nothing that made any sense to me. I just knew that I had to protect my mother and keep her from being beaten, so we had to run. Jacksonville was pitch black at night, with no lights on anywhere to tell us where we were going. I had no idea where we were going , only that it was just far enough away from Daddy, so that he couldn't beat her up. We ran and ran and ran. I was puffing, breathing heavy, and Mamma was sweating.

After we were several blocks away, I finally looked up at her and asked, "Why don't you get a divorce? People shouldn't live like this." Divorce was not a household word in the early forties. People did get divorced, but it was not talked about and it was a disgrace. So at eight or nine I don't know where I knew about divorce, but I knew people were not meant to live the way we were living.

My mother looked at me perplexed as if no one had ever suggested that she could do something different. I understand that when my mother first married my father her family was not pleased. Her family was a professional family, her father was a surgeon and my father had a reputation of being pretty "fast." He was ten years older than my mother and had been married once before had and a little girl was born from that union. I was an adult before I ever knew this, so I don't know what he ever did about his first daughter.

Mamma and I went to a hotel. I kept wondering, "How did she know to go there, where did the money come from to pay for it?" Mamma never had any money. There were lots of questions I couldn't answer. We went into a room and fell on the bed. I still couldn't go to sleep, but Mamma was very tired and fell asleep. I drifted off to sleep, but I woke up first and started screaming, "Daddy's been in here, are you hurt, mother, Mamma, wake up, I think you are hurt."

Mamma woke up, shushing me, telling me to be quiet and I put my fingers in my mouth and cried. She cuddled me and laughing said "No, your daddy hasn't been here, what do you mean?"

I was looking at her face all pock-marked, black dots all over her face. I knew that he had been hitting her, but the marks were different. I said, "What are those marks on your face?"

She got up from the bed and looked in the mirror then started laughing. I still didn't see anything funny.

"We left the window open last night and when the train passed by, the cinders flew in and the screen on the window made the marks on my face."

After a few months in Jacksonville, we moved to West Palm Beach and were there only a few weeks. We moved up and down the east coast of Florida. I went to five different schools in the fifth grade. We averaged moving every six weeks. I learned to smile during this period of time. I was always the new kid on the block and learned that if I smiled the kids didn't bother me too much. It was always hurry up and catch-up with the new curriculum and learning the new teacher's technique. In West Palm Beach (we moved there twice so, I went to school there twice) my Aunt Mary, the one who sent the clothes to Aunt Myrtle, was a truant officer, so she told us kids in no uncertain words that we better not mess up. Of course, I didn't have to worry about me, but I sure worried a lot about Roy. He was already beginning to skip school, get into trouble and put Daddy into a bigger rage. I just tried to keep up. Jack was somewhere around, but being a quiet kid who was sick a lot, he didn't give anybody any trouble. I have often wished I knew what my brothers thought of all these episodes, but both of them are dead and I will never know. Roy was murdered in 1981, and Jack died in 1996. Up to and until his death, Roy was a very disturbed person. He was in and out of prison, married five times, had many live-ins and had many relationships gone sour. He had four sons that I know about but to my knowledge never contributed to their support or welfare in any way. But I may be wrong. I don't know. Jack, on the other hand, was married to the one and only wife he ever had, had a son and a daughter, worked and provided very well for his family. I hope they remember him with love and kindness as I do.

———•———

When I was ten, we were in Griffin, Georgia. Daddy was now the pastor at a Baptist church. We were living in a large house that had several apartments, so the evenings were nice when all the families went out on the porch and we laughed and talked. I seemed to be the brunt of Daddy's jokes and being the shy kid I was I didn't realize his kidding was of a loving nature. I just knew I didn't know the words he was using to describe my actions. He would tell all the people sitting on the porch that he saw me "hesitating" at the corner. They would all laugh, calling out, "Janis, you didn't," and I would hang my head and put my fingers in my mouth. He said he watched me vacillate at the playground or that I had masticated at the dinner table. This was all said to great laughter and knee slapping. My face would turn beet-red, my heart pounding, because I didn't know what those words meant. To top it off, though, he said, "Did you know Jan slumbers in her bed?" Being a bed wetter until I was twelve, I just knew this had something to do with my shame of all shames. Now all the neighbors knew. My shame knew no end. This would go on forever it seemed like and everyone would laugh and I would cringe. The war was still going on and entertainment was what you made of it. Now I understand that Daddy was doing this out of loving humor, but at the time I didn't know when he would turn and be mad about something.

While Daddy was the pastor at the church, Mamma was taking care of kids and the house. We had moved into the parsonage next to the church. I was very active in GA's (Girl's Auxiliary), Sunday school, and the Sunday evening youth group. At the age of twelve I accepted the call. Jack and I were baptized by our father, and Our Father. I felt very grown up taking on such an act of responsibility. I felt that I was even more accountable for my actions. I felt guilty about everything, which meant that I was not really up to the task of talking care of everything and everyone. But how valiantly I tried.

We were fortunate that our parents wanted us to have our friends over. After church on Sundays there would be several kids to eat Sunday dinner with us. We would sit in the closed-off dark, musty parlor, which was the nicest room in the house. One afternoon when we had finished eating we were sitting in the living room, listening to the radio. This was our favorite pastime. My brother Roy had a boy over, Sweetie, who was a few years older than I. I had such a crush on him that I was stumbling over my tongue, and of course I wanted to impress him. I don't remember what I said or what the subject was but I used the word *darn*. I blushed and ran from the room, crying. I went to my room and cried for the rest of the afternoon knowing that I was going to hell for using such a bad word.

For the next few years we lived on in Griffin, Georgia. I went there in the fifth grade and completed seventh grade before we moved out of the area. I still went to several schools.

I started my period in the seventh grade and was mortified. My mother came to school and took me home. She put me to bed, built a big fire in the bedroom, plumped up the pillows, and I stayed in bed for the next several days. I wasn't sick, but I figured that there must have been something more that I was not aware of for her to turn me into an invalid. I liked the attention but didn't like the new "visitor" that came to me once a month.

My father changed churches, and we were now commuting to The Rock Baptist Church in Rex, Georgia, which was about forty miles from Griffin. It was on the outskirts of Atlanta. We went there two or three times a week before we finally moved into the parsonage. While we were commuting I was finishing up seventh grade. We moved and Daddy began a tour of pastoring. We were very involved with church, always going to church , going, several times a week.

I went to eighth grade in Jonesboro, Georgia, where *Gone With The Wind* wassupposedly filmed. There was the big house, Tara, and rumor had it that the house was "just a shell."

Again I was the new kid on the block. It didn't take too long before I was busy with school, singing in the glee club, a member of different clubs. Once a year the school elected two girls from each grade to represent their grade, and a competition was held to pick which girl would be crowned queen. This was decided by each girl collecting pennies and whoever collected the most pennies was the winner. I was elected for my eighth grade class. I was so excited I could hardly stand it. There was some talk around that the girls elected were the prettiest in their class. I couldn't believe that was true, but whatever the truth I was elected. I was given a decorated jar and told to get the pennies. Pennies from heaven?

I rushed home, as fast as you can rush riding the school bus, and flew in the door hollering, "Mamma, Daddy, come quick. I have something to tell you. You won't believe what happened!"

My parents came into the living room where I was yelling and said, "Quiet down, Jan, people will hear you and what will the neighbors think?"

"Okay, okay, but let me tell you what happened. See, they have this thing at school…"

Daddy was frowning. This was not going the way I wanted it to go. But I plunged forward.

"Daddy, please," I started begging.

He was frowning, shaking his head no. He didn't even know what I was going to say, and he was already nixing the idea.

My mother said, "Obie, let her tell her us what it is. Tell us."

"At school, they have a program that assists the school in getting equipment that the school board can't afford. This year it is equipment for the football team and glee club. And they elected me to represent the eighth grade. They also say it's for the prettiest girl in the class, but I don't think that's true." I paused for a few seconds, trying to determine what Daddy was thinking. His face was blank with his brown piercing eyes staring at me.

"And what we do is we have this decorated jar and the girl that gets the most votes wins and the winner in each grade gets a prize, like candy or some treats. I can't believe they chose me since this is my first year and I'm so new in school. I didn't know anyone knew me." I slowed down for a minute.

"How do you get these votes," Daddy asked.

We collect a penny a vote and when the three weeks are up we turn in our pennies and the one with the most pennies collected is the winner. "Daddy will you vote for me?" I asked.

Daddy's face turned crimson; his eyes flashed. I knew that look and now I was scared. What on earth had I done or said that had brought on this latest siege of rage?

"No daughter of mine will ever take money from anybody! Do you hear me? Never! Take that jar back; tell them you are not allowed to do such a stupid, cheap trick. You are my daughter and you will not collect money." He was raging now and throwing his hands around, saliva seeping at the corners of his mouth.

"Obie, let's hear more of what Janis has to say. Don't stop her now; let's hear the rest," Mamma pleaded.

"There is no more to hear."

With that Daddy stomped out of the house, got in his new Buick and left. I wanted to explain but was afraid he wouldn't be back. But this was like so many other times when he left me standing at the slammed door, with my fingers in my mouth, crying my heart out.

Mamma put her arms around me and I cried. Again I would have to tell some school official that I could not participate in the school programs. The previous year in Griffin we were suppose to go to movies as a class project. My brother Jack was in another class and his class was going also. Jack and I went home excited about going to the movies and about doing activities with the school. "No. No," we could not go. "It is a sin to go to the movies," Daddy proclaimed. No discussion. Jack and I were humiliated to tell the teacher and other kids we could not go.

I cried the rest of the afternoon. I put the decorated jar down with my school things and shut-off the enthusiasm I had for school, for life. It was such an effort to keep up a positive attitude around my dad. That is, unless he wanted me to be positive, then, on cue, I had to be positive.

———•———

I started wearing hose, small high heels, and dressing like a lady. I was fourteen and tall. I loved school, especially the library. I often heard, "You have your nose in a book again. You don't do anything, you are lazy, and I don't understand what you get out of those books."

We moved several more times, and I finally graduated from high school in 1950. Daddy would not allow me to work and he would not allow me to go to college, although my English teacher obtained a scholarship for me. Daddy said, "There are too many sinners there, you can't go."

I wasn't allowed to date, although Daddy let me go to my senior prom with a boy from the church whom I didn't really like. Daddy said I didn't need to go out with boys, "You're better off home with me and your mamma." Why? So I could hear them yelling at each other?

Daddy had resigned as pastor of the church and decided to go on the road preaching and saving souls. It was decided that I would go with him.

4

Sopchoppy

Members bought and donated the benches and the tent. Daddy's plan was to travel from town to town, pitch his tent, set it up with benches, build a platform and save souls. He would do this and be successful to a degree until he fell from Grace one more time from the same insatiable appetite.

Part of Daddy's plan was for a piano to go with him. And for me to go along and play it.

I wasn't too happy about the prospect of being away from my friends and my mother. Mamma traveled with us some of the time, but again, she and Daddy were not getting along well.

She didn't go often. So Daddy, the tent, the benches, the piano, and I toured small towns in south Georgia and north and central Florida. We started off pretty inexperienced, but gradually learned the ropes. The names of the places we visited escape me now. We sometimes lost track of the names of the places even when we were there. Two weeks was usually the time in each place, then on to another town.

Daddy was sought after. People from different towns would come, hear him preach and ask him to come to their town. Frequently he was asked to go to a church and hold revival meetings. Then we would store the tent and go stay in a small town for two to three weeks. One of those places was Sopchoppy, in the panhandle of Florida. There weren't palm trees but a lot of palmetto bushes, pine trees and sand. Sopchoppy is a little fishing village with just a couple of bait stores, a service station, and a Baptist church. We were invited to Sopchoppy for two to three weeks to hold services at the Baptist church. We were given a fishing cottage to stay in and part of the collection each night. The money was not abundant on the evangelical circuit.

Many times I had heard Daddy cry and plead with the congregation to donate money, or he would have to fold his tent and steal away in the night. He would have to give up saving souls, and North Florida and South Georgia would surely go straight to hell. The prospect of being at a place for two weeks with a free place to stay, fed by the church members, and part of the collection was too good to turn down. There were several businessmen who believed in my daddy and they donated money to keep us in food and board. Mamma kept the home fires burning and would make an appearance, periodically.

Daddy was excited and, as was Daddy's pattern, "When I'm happy, everybody's happy," prevailed. We were making preparations to go to Sopchoppy when Daddy realized how lonely I would be. It was difficult to make girlfriends my age when we were in and out of all the towns so quickly. I had a special girlfriend who attended Eastside Baptist Church, and Daddy asked her to join us

Alma was a year older, about my height, a little heavier, had dishwater blond hair and wore glasses. None of the boys at church thought she was pretty, but I liked her because she was nice to me. She was a friend to me. Daddy offered her ten dollars a week to travel with us and be my "companion." But he decided that Alma should sing and lead the singing while I played. I had had about four months of sporadic piano lessons; Alma had never had a singing lesson in her life. And I must say, Alma sang no better than I played.

We three arrived at Sopchoppy and went directly to our "home away from home" to freshen up before the service began. The cabin was a typical fishing cabin, functional but sparse. There were three rooms and a bath. The first room was Alma's and my bedroom. It contained a double bed and a dresser. The other room was smaller, but it had a bed in it, and that's where Daddy stayed. There was a kitchen but we didn't use that much.

The weather was lovely as it can be in North Florida during the fall months. We were welcomed and were dined morning, noon and night; each meal at a different place. We were offered deep-sea fishing jaunts, boat trips and all the seafood we could eat. We were sure we were in heaven. Little did I know that soon it would turn into a living hell.

Daddy had begun to loosen his grip on me somewhat, and I was allowed to go off with some of the young church members occasionally. There were comments made everywhere about how Daddy would soon be losing me because "a young pretty girl like Sister Janis is going to up and marry on you, Brother Guest." I couldn't imagine getting married and surely not to any of those hayseeds. I hated standing in line after each service and having those old men come up and hug me. They smelled bad, they rubbed their hands up my back like they were petting me, and I especially hated being called "Sister Janis." I didn't know anything about sex, yet I intuitively knew these old men had more on their mind than their souls. My brother Jack, who was three years older than I, was working and living in Iowa, and he decided to come home for a few weeks. In order to be with me and to have some of Daddy's time, Jack came to Florida. We had fun fishing and being together. Alma liked Jack and was interested in getting a romance going, but Jack wasn't interested in Alma.

Daddy talked to Jack about Alma and told him what a nice girl Alma was and what a good Christian girl she was. Jack still wasn't interested. There was a boy about my age named Clyde. Clyde's daddy owned a marina and a fishing camp. They were big supporters of the church and were instrumental in getting Daddy to hold a revival at their church.

Clyde had access to all the boats and gear that we needed for fishing or picnicking. I had never been oystering, although I loved to eat them, raw or otherwise. Jack, Alma, Clyde and I got the boat out after church services one night and went oystering. Daddy even encouraged my being with Clyde, and I couldn't understand that at all. Clyde was fat, his face was pockmarked and he was never neatly dressed. To me he was repulsive, but I still went oystering with him. The night was clear, a big moon was shining and the temperature was brisk, but not cold. Clyde knew where the oyster beds were, and in no time we were anchored on one of the beds. The oyster beds looked as if someone had taken a hundred buckets of oyster shells and dumped them all in one place. That's basically what happens, except that oysters in beds spawn and new oysters grow and new shells come and on and on and on. The moon was like a big floor lamp lighting the living room of the bay when we started out. We were all laughing and talking enjoying my brother and Alma. I was trying to forget Clyde was there, although he was nice enough to take us out in his boat. We had some cold drinks, saltine crackers and the indispensable Tobasco sauce to eat with the oysters. Just as I was trying to be Christian and think nice thoughts about Clyde, he pulled out a pack of Juicy Fruit gum and said, "Here, take this and sweeten up your breath."

Even though he gave Jack and Alma some too, I wanted to jump overboard and drown from humiliation. Did we all have bad breath? And if we did, how could he be so crude as to mention it? On the way back Clyde told Jack to handle the boat. Clyde moved up in the bow where I was and tried to fondle me. I told him in no uncertain terms that Christian love didn't extend to him, and I didn't care if he was never saved! Our little group went back to the marina a little quieter. Clyde attempted to talk to me, but I wasn't interested. Finally he said, "Guess your daddy's gonna' havta' talk to you! My daddy done talked to your daddy and your daddy said, 'Good, it's okay with him.'"

Mentioning my daddy caught my attention and I said, "What? What are you talking about?"

"My daddy done ast your daddy if I could marry you and your daddy said yes. There now — I weren't 'pose to tell you but there. I done did it."

In the pale moonlight I looked at Clyde and yelled as loudly as I could "You liar! My daddy didn't say I could marry anyone! Let alone you!" I was dying inside.

My brother Jack said, "Hush, Jan. Someone might hear us. And what would people think?"

At that moment I didn't care. Again I wanted to jump overboard and drown. Although I calmed down outwardly, inside I was a bucket of clenched nerves. Could it be possible my daddy was involved in such a conspiracy? I know it was unusual for Daddy to let me go as freely as he had in Sopchoppy, yet I thought he knew how repulsed I was by Clyde and that was why he didn't say anything about our running around together. 'Nothing to worry about," I told myself.

We docked, cleaned up the boat and went home in silence. Daddy was asleep when we got in, so we quietly went to bed.

The next day was busy with visiting the sick, calling on shut-ins and getting ready for the evening service. We were also busy saying goodbye to Jack. I was sad to see him go. I felt close to my brother, but our closeness didn't include talking. We didn't discuss my feelings about Daddy telling Clyde's daddy that I would marry him. A couple of days later I asked Daddy if it was true what Clyde said.

"Jan baby, he's going to own all of this marina one day. his daddy told me he would give Clyde anything he wanted if you married him. He's not so bad, Clyde. He's going to be rich, Jan baby."

I watched him with bile rising in my throat. Surely he wasn't serious. Surely he was talking about something else. Yet something nasty and squirmy in the pit of my stomach told me it was true. There was something in this for Daddy. How much money had Clyde's daddy offered my daddy to sell me? That's what it amounted to, Daddy selling me.

"Daddy, I don't ever want to get married. Now or ever! To Clyde especially. And maybe you need to ask me before you sell me again."

"Oh, Jan baby, you know that's not true. It's just that he'll be okay, Clyde will."

I walked out of the cottage. I couldn't look at my daddy anymore. It was all so confusing to me. If Daddy wouldn't let me date Gene, someone I liked, while we were in high school, why would he be so free with me now? As I walked away, I began to think back about six or eight months before. Something strange had happened, and now it was becoming clearer.

We were at a church in Adel, another small town in South Georgia for a three-week revival. One of the church members was an elderly lady who was supportive of Daddy and his ministry. Mrs. Vinson owned a large farm, with acres planted in tobacco, corn and other crops. She was a widow, and her son, Sonny, lived with her and managed the farm. Sonny was old, at least to my sixteen-year-old eyes. He was around thirty-five, six feet tall or more, with brown hair and eyes, a handsome man. I noticed that he stayed after the services and usually came up to speak to me. I also noticed that Daddy talked a good deal about Mrs. Vinson and Sonny, saying things like, "Sonny sure runs that farm good, "I wonder how many acres Mrs. Vinson has, that Sonny sure will be fixed when his momma dies." None of this made a difference to me; I was off in my dream world. I was so unsophisticated that I wasn't aware of what was going on.

One night after church Sonny came up to me and asked if he could take me home. I didn't hear him, so he had to repeat it. "I sure would like to take you home. Brother Guest said it's okay."

I just stared at him thinking he's crazy. Daddy would never let me get in a car with him, a thirty-five-year-old man. Six months earlier Daddy wouldn't let me ride on the bus with the football team, band members and chaperones for a high school football game out of town. Why would he let me drive forty miles with this old man?

"Can Alma come with us?"

"Sure, she can even drive my new Buick," Sonny said, grinning like the whale that swallowed Jonah.

I went up to Daddy and asked, "Did you tell Sonny Vinson he could take me home?"

"Uh, sure, honey, Sonny can drive you home. He's a nice man. He's got a new Buick. But you go right home, you hear?"

Daddy didn't look at me, he was busy shaking hands and giving *God bless-yous.*

I called to Alma to come with us. We went out to the car, the new Buick, and Sonny said, "Alma, how 'bout you drive, and me and Jan can sit in the backseat.

Alma's eyes got huge at the thought of driving a Buick.

"No, we can all three sit up front," I quickly replied. I didn't want to sit in the back with him. There was something about him that frightened me, maybe because he was seventeen years older than I was. I just knew that something wasn't quite right.

Sonny opened the back door and we got in. As we moved, I was so frightened. Alma was a good driver, but she was so excited that her driving was erratic. She went from side to side, enough to make Sonny fall over next to me. Actually, I think that Sonny was doing more of the movement on his own than Alma was with the car.

Georgia nights frequently are pitch black. No illumination from moon, stars or headlights. Nothing. Just a black tunnel. We went down the highway, Alma concentrated on her driving, and I concentrated on — what? I wasn't concentrating. I was poised for flight. I didn't like being in the back seat or any other seat with Sonny. There was an aura, a vibration, something that made me wary.

"You sure are pretty, Jan," Sonny breathed hotly in my ear. I moved closer into the side of the car, next to the door. Pretty soon I would be outside if he kept pushing. He moved closer.

Taking my left hand into his, he said, "You're so pretty, and so pure. You're so godly, so pure."

I didn't want him to hold my hand, it felt dirty. His hands were wet, and his breath on the side of my face was hot. I tried to pull my hand away but he held on. "Please, Janis," he breathed.

I hated the name Janis, and please what? What was he saying? My mind was darting and diving from one thought to another. At that moment I hated Sonny and, frighteningly, I hated Daddy. I never allowed bad thoughts to come into my mind about Daddy. If I did he might leave again, might 'en he? I just wanted out of that car and to be home.

Suddenly Sonny swooped sideways. I was engulfed in his arms with a vise-like grip. I couldn't move. I was in a panic, yet too scared to yell at Alma. Before I could move away, Sonny's hot breath and mouth were covering mine. I opened my mouth to yell and his tongue pushed through my mouth like a torpedo to a target. I began to kick, breaking his hold, and I gagged. He pulled back from me and tried to pat my head, pat my back, just fluttering little movements with his hands. Now the life was back in me, and Daddy or no Daddy, Sonny or no Sonny, money or not, I wouldn't accept this treatment. I yelled at him to get away from me and never touch me again. He apologized and tried to be sweet, still trying to hold my hand, but I wouldn't let him touch me, nor would I talk to him. The rest of the trip was completed in silence. Alma never said a word, she just drove. The next day Daddy asked me how the ride home was. I didn't dare tell him about Sonny's behavior. "I don't like him, Daddy," I said. "He's too old."

Daddy didn't say anything, and that was the end of that. But it all was clear in my mind as I thought about the development with Clyde. Why would Daddy want me to be with men I couldn't stand and not let me date boys I liked? It didn't make sense.

The Sopchoppy revival was going along okay, but the internal upheaval was taking its toll on me. I was quiet, lethargic, and sad; most of all sad. I didn't know how to comprehend all of this. I loved Daddy. He was a good man, preaching the gospel, saving souls, yet there was something not in harmony. It was as if Daddy's soul was a symphony, but the orchestra was playing a folk tune. It was all out of sync.

———•———

We had completed the first week of the revival and were starting on the second. Reverend Eustas Clay was supposed to come hold the services with us, as all three of us were tired and in need of a break. We had been getting good crowds all along, and this night with Reverend Clay was no exception. Alma and I were better in our music that night, and there was an air of excitement. We played the up tempo hymns that I liked: *There's Power in the Blood, I'll Fly Away, Just a Little Talk with Jesus,* and *Just a Little While.* We were smoking!

Reverend Clay preached fire and brimstone and that we were all going to hell. He was fired up, yelling and hollering about the wages of sin. He jumped around the podium, flailing his arms, socking his fist into the palm of his other hand. He ran from one end of the platform to the other. The brothers and sisters were crying out "Amens" and "Yes, brothers." He had the congregation in the palm of his hand and knew it. He was on a roll. He grabbed the rough, orange crate built pulpit with both hands. He jumped up, flinging his right leg to transcend the pulpit. A sharp nail at the corner of the crate snagged his pants, piercing his leg. Blood spurted out reminding me of the lambs my uncle butchered.

Reverend Clay jumped back, grasping his leg, hopping around like a one-legged chicken. "Oh, shit . . . oh, godda . . . oh, hallelujah, oh shit, oh praise God, oh, hell, God, somebody help me," and he fell down. Alma and I looked at each other, knowing it shouldn't be funny, but we had a hard time keeping straight faces. A signal from Daddy and I started softly playing *Just As I Am*. I thought it was fitting.

Daddy finished the service by laying hands on Reverend Clay and asking the congregation to pray for his soul. Satan was in him, but Daddy would smite the devil out of his fellow reverend.

—————•—————

We had been told there was unrest in the community. Some hoodlums were drinking too much and causing problems. We weren't too concerned because it really didn't disrupt our little world, or so we thought. Wednesday nights were usually a little more strenuous on us than other weeknights because more people often attended Wednesday night prayer meetings at the church. We worked hard, had a good service, and several people answered the call. The call to be saved and accept Jesus Christ as their Savior. We came away from church tired but feeling good. Daddy was going deep-sea fishing the next morning at six o'clock, so we three went to bed early. Alma and I talked for a little while, about boys, naturally, but we soon went to sleep. My sleeping had been sporadic for as long as I could remember. "Jan's lazy," teachers or others would say because I couldn't go to sleep at night and would be sleepy the next morning. For most of my life, my sleep was disrupted at some point during the night. This night was no different.

I awoke, startled, because the bed was shaking. I lay there for a moment, trying to fathom what was going on. It was very dark, and I slowly opened my eyes to see what was happening. I couldn't see anything; I just felt the bed as it kept moving. I reached over and touched Alma on the arm. "What's going on?" I asked. I could tell then that Alma was crying. I whispered to her, "What's wrong? Why are you crying?"

Alma sobbed quietly. "Go back to sleep. We'll talk tomorrow."

"No, Alma. Tell me now. What's wrong?" I whispered more loudly.

"Shhh, Brother Guest will hear us. Go back to sleep." She was still crying but less violently.

That all-too-familiar bucket of worms in my guts started squirming around and the bile started rising in my throat. I felt sick. I felt angry. I was horrified, but I asked anyway.

"Did my father mess with you, Alma?"

Alma started shaking so hard I thought the bed would walk out of that little cottage with us on it. She was crying and shaking like she would never stop. I didn't know what to do.

How could Daddy do this? I didn't know yet what Daddy had done, but I knew intuitively that it was something sexual.

"Go back to sleep, Jan. Brother Guest has to get up early for his fishing trip," she said trying to smother her sobs.

"Did he, Alma? Answer me. Did my daddy do anything to you?" I grated out the questions, like a Gestapo interrogator. I no longer cared if we made noise, or woke Daddy, or if he went fishing.

"Please, Jan. Don't make me talk anymore. Go back to sleep," Alma said. Alma, the thoughtful one, the one always concerned about others, and here, true to form, she was concerned about my daddy.

"Tell me if he did and I'll leave you alone," I said as I shook her arm.

"Yes," she barely whispered, starting the crying and shaking again.

"What did he do?" I almost yelled.

"You promised, Jan. You promised if I told you, you would go back to sleep. I'll tell you in the morning. But I'm afraid Brother Guest is going to hear us and come in here." She continued to sob and shake.

"Oh, Alma. I did promise, but you promise you'll tell me what happened in the morning?" I squeezed her arm.

"Yes, I promise."

How, I don't know, but we both slept. I vaguely remember hearing Daddy leaving the next morning for his deep-sea fishing trip. He was supposed to be gone until noon, so Alma and I would have plenty of time to talk.

I must have slept longer than I thought because when I woke up Alma said Daddy had come back early. She said he spoke to her when he came through the room; he told her that he was sick.

I was sick myself, but I asked her to tell me what had happened. We spoke quietly. She was calmer and wasn't shaking or crying.

"Last night I went to sleep after we talked. I was tired and I was in a deep sleep when I thought I was dreaming that a dog was licking my feet. I thought that was strange. Then I became aware that I wasn't dreaming. It was Preacher Guest at the end of the bed licking my feet. Then his hands moved up my legs. I sat up, and he put both hands on my breasts. Then I started crying and whispering, 'No, Preacher Guest, no.'

"I was afraid I would wake you. He then started trying to kiss me and saying please let him please let him that Sister...Guest never let him. I cried and said, no, Preacher Guest, please no. You're going to wake up Jan. With that he just turned around and went back to his room."

She had poured all of that out like a torrent of rain. She no longer cried or showed much emotion.

I felt like a volcano about to erupt. And I did. I jumped out of bed yelling, "Get up. Get dressed. I'm going to call my father in here. Both of you had better get one thing straight."

Alma began to cry and said, "No, Jan. Let Brother Guest sleep. He's sick from the deep-sea fishing."

I glared at her. Wasn't she at fault, too, someway?

I didn't know, but I knew I had to do one thing. I rushed into Daddy's room, no knock, no calling out, just marched in. "Daddy, get up! Get dressed and come into the other room. I want to talk to you!"

"Oh, Jan baby," he moaned. "I'm so sick."

"You're sick all right but get up and get dressed," I spat out at him.

"I've got to stay in bed for a while," he groaned, "Oh, Jan baby, the sea was so rough, and I'm so sick."

"You're sick but not from the sea," I snapped. "Get dressed!" I stomped out of his room. Alma was dressed in a faded yellow dress and looked like a bleached oak trunk. She was pale. Her hair was stringy and her eyes wide behind her coke-bottle thick glasses. She looked scared. Daddy came into the room, trousers and suspenders over his blue, rumpled pajamas. My daddy was known for his starched white shirts and dark, satin ties. He was never seen disheveled other than when fishing. His face had a green cast, and I noticed a slight trembling.

I was fixing my hair at the mirror over the dresser. Looking in the mirror at both of them I said, "I want you both to listen and listen good.

I know what went on last night and if either of you ever, ever tells my mother I'll kill you!"

They both just stared at me. I meant what I said, "My mother will not be hurt anymore," not if I could help it, anyway. "Do you hear me? Do you hear what I said? If either of you says a word about this to my mother I will kill you!" I was mad and I knew they knew it.

"Oh, Jan baby," said Daddy as he slunk back off to bed.

That night at the closing of the service I played, *There's Power in the Blood*. The rest of the day we three went about our duties as though nothing had happened. As though we were on a holiday jaunt where the sun shines but never too hot, and the night rain only washes away the day's grime. But we weren't on holiday. We were God's chosen shepherds sent to bring the flock to Him. Why on God's earth were we entangled in carnal sin?

That night at church a couple of the older ladies commented that I looked pale. I wasn't getting sick, was I? I lied and said, "No, just tired." How could I say what was wrong? I didn't speak that language; the language of feelings, of truth.

The service was subdued, none of us brought the energy and excitement of Reverend Clay's pierced leg. We closed the service and, for a change, we didn't go to someone's home for cake and coffee. Daddy begged off "because he thought he was coming down with the flu." We were tired, physically, emotionally and spiritually. I was so confused about God and His love and man and his love. I loved my daddy, but I also hated him. And wasn't hate a sin? And didn't the Bible say, "Honor thy Mother and Father?" I did my mother, God bless the saint, but I was having trouble with my father.

Oh, Jan baby," said Daddy as he slunk back off to bed.

We were almost asleep when Alma and I heard some cars pull up into the driveway. It was too late for visitors, so the only other thing it could be was as an emergency. A few times, when someone got sick or there was an accident, we would go and pray for the injured, but tonight sounded different. There were a lot of voices and several car doors slamming.

"Come on out, Preacher," a male voice called.

"Yeah, Pree-cher," a voice mocked, putting great emphasis on his name.

"Come on Preach, bring your secretaries." Laughter came crashing through the cottage like angry waves accosting the jetties.

Alma and I were rigid with fright. We couldn't move and we were afraid to speak. Daddy was in the next room—was he asleep?

"Come on Reverend, let us see your pretty daughter and your secretary. We know you're in there," fists pounded on the door, voices cut through the beams.

"Yeah your sect—reee-taary!" mocked another voice.

"An your dau—u—ughter-er-er, sure your daughter. We know about men like you, claiming the name of God as your cover-up."

"We know how you praise God, while you're doing *it* to your *secretaries*," laughed another.

"We know those girls with you are whores. That's not your daughter. All a secretary is good for is to screw her." This was a different voice, with a maniacal laugh and a thick hillbilly accent.

How many men were there? Alma and I could not tell. They changed their voices with mocking, mimicking, soft then loud, seductive and threatening phrases. We listened to this hurricane of voices, feeling we were in the eye of the storm. Would they huff and puff and blow our house down, damning our souls to hell? Did they know Daddy had tried to seduce Alma? And then the God-awful realization swept over me like the last gust of a hurricane. Daddy must have tried, maybe even succeeded, to seduce other women in the church community. The wife or girlfriend of one of these men? Had Daddy's reputation preceded him? The same bucket of worms was eating away at my guts. What if these men broke in? Would they kill us? Would they kill Daddy, "have their way" with me and Alma?

Alama and I were the virgins of the 1950s. We had never been with a man in the *biblical sense*. I had hardly been in a boy/girl relationship. "God protect us," I prayed. "Get us out of this mess."

Pretty soon the banging on the door, the beating on the wooden walls of the cottage and the caterwauling stopped. One of the men said, "Ah, they must not be in there. The preacher is probably out in the woods with both of them."

With the mention of that, the men started running their mouths, describing their fantasies of the preacher with two young girls. One pretending to be "the secretary," another pretending to be, me, the preacher's daughter. Their truck engines started; the noise was like the start of the Indianapolis 500, then they were gone.

Our rigid bodies began to relax, and without a word about what had just happened, we drifted off to sleep. The next morning I asked Daddy, "Did you hear that racket last night?"

"Yes baby," he said. "They were just a bunch of drunks. I wouldn't let them come in. I'm a man of God." Then he left to pray over a man who was dying. Would he tell that man not to question or ask why?

Mr. Presley was a staunch supporter of Daddy's and did whatever Daddy told him to do. Mr. Presley handled all of the logistics of the revivals so Daddy was free to save souls. Mr. Presley also contributed more than what came into the collection plates. Finally, the two consulted, and decided that they had saved all of the souls they could in Sopchoppy. We closed the revival the next day, Sunday. Alma and I were tired physically, but more than fatigued, we were soul sick. I know I was, even without being able to verbalize it or label it. I felt betrayed with that all too familiar sense of abandonment. I felt God and all humankind had left me.

We went home. We walked through the door, and my mother screamed and ran to me. "What have you done to her? My God, what have you done?" She was on the verge of tears. She was looking accusingly at Daddy.

I put my bag down and hugged her. "I'm okay Mamma, just tired."

"Well come in here and let me fix you something to eat, and then you get yourself up to bed. You look near to death's door." She walked into the kitchen not saying another word to Daddy.

After pushing some food around on the plate I excused myself and went to bed. I fell into a troubled, restless sleep. Were the angry, shouting voices real, or another bad dream? For days I was lethargic, listless and (a word I didn't know at the time) depressed. Was I bad? Was I an abomination in the sight of God? I didn't know, but I felt guilty. Had I done something wrong to make Daddy act like he did? What was it? What had I done?

Alma and I caught up on our rest and a few days after we were home, she was over at my house. We had not spoken of our experiences in Sopchoppy.

Mamma, Alma and I were talking about clothes. "Go get your blue cotton blouse I made for you to show Alma," my mother said. "If she likes it, maybe I can make her one."

I went upstairs knowing that I could put my hand on my blue blouse. It was in the center of my closet, hanging with my blue and white print skirt, my favorite outfit. I opened my closet door, no blue blouse, just the skirt. It was strange. I looked around on the floor. My mother often said I was messy and left my clothes on the floor of the closet, but no blouse. I looked on the floor. After several minutes I decided to go downstairs to ask Mother if she had moved it, when my foot hit something under the edge of my bed. I knelt down and picked up the blouse still on the hanger.

As I walked through the living room, I noticed my mother stroking Alma's hair and saying, "It's okay, don't worry." Alma had her glasses off and looked as if she had been crying.

"Mamma, why was my blouse under the bed?"

"What, your blouse? Oh Jan, you know how messy and irresponsible you are. You probably put it under there because you were too lazy to hang it up. Now go hang it up properly."

"Don't you want Alma to try it on to see if she likes it so you can make her one?" I was stung by her criticism, knowing I had not shoved my blouse under the bed.

"She doesn't like it; it's not her style. You are just a little girl and your clothes are too babyish for her. Now go!" My mother sounded like she was mad at me, and at the world. Now what had I done? I needed so desperately to be a good little girl. I tried, but what was happening?

Alma just looked down at her feet like all the riddles of life were explained down there.

Later Alma and I went down to Minnix's Drugstore to get a soda. Alma had sweet lemonade; I had lemon juice, soda water and salt. She sat across the booth from me, looking as if she had lost her best friend, but here I was her best friend, sitting right across from her.

"Alma, what is it?" I asked. "What's wrong with you?"

"Oh Jan, why didn't you tell me you told your mother what happened in Sopchoppy? Why did you tell her after you said you would kill us if she ever found out? Why didn't you tell me?" Alma was almost in tears.

I stared at her dumbfounded. I truly felt like the "dumb, little country girl," I was so often told I was. "Alma, are you saying that my mother told you she knew what happened in Sopchoppy?"

"Yes. She said to me, 'Jan told me what happened down there, but why don't you tell me because you know Jan, she always leaves something out.' She said, 'I know it was hard on you, but you'll feel better if you talk it out.' Oh Jan, I was scared, but you know, she was right, I did feel better after I talked about it." Alma sighed.

"Alma, my mother tricked you. I didn't tell her anything," I fought back the tears. I didn't understand. Again I felt confused, all was not right with the home with which I should have felt familiar, but did not. Was I upset now because Mamma knew about Daddy, or because I was beginning to recognize the manipulative trait that my mother possessed?

"What do you mean she tricked me, Jan?" Alma blinked hard through her thick glasses. "Sister Guest wouldn't trick me."

At that moment I hated Alma, I hated everybody. "Alma does this sound familiar?" I mimicked my mother's voice and said, "Jan told me what happened, but why don't you tell me?" I yelled at Alma, "Alma can't you see my mother tricked you? I told her nothing."

I got up from the booth, walked towards the door, dropped my quarter next to the cash register and left. I had had enough of Alma, Daddy, Mother and God.

5

From Girl to Woman

I graduated from high school in Moultrie, Georgia, in 1950. It was a great but mixed up time for me. Great in that I was the first one in my family to graduate from high school. Mixed up because I was a very naive, unsophisticated little girl and scared. Scared, but with a strength and determination I didn't know I had.

I know that life in the 1950s is very different from the 21st century. It's also a different world in morals, values, behavior, and more openness. Now, anything goes or so it seems, but in the 1950's, life was portrayed as simpler, kinder, and more contained. People didn't go on national TV and tell their most intimate thoughts and feelings. Feelings? It was not a word used in the 1950s. Not a word used as it is today. The truth was that I knew nothing about feelings. The few times I said what I thought or felt, I was told that I shouldn't feel or think that way and that I was stupid for saying things about feelings.

When I was accepted by American Airlines as a stewardess in 1955, I was ecstatic and scared. Most of my life has been lived with fear and I didn't know if I could handle the demanding work in stewardess college or if I was smart enough. And I certainly wasn't pretty enough, which was the real mystery to my having been accepted. Having heard all of my life that I was "stupid, dumb and ugly," I had no belief in myself, yet somewhere in the core of my being I knew I would make it.

I arrived at Midway Airport, Chicago, March 1955, on a foggy, cold day. The airport was in frenzy with workers cleaning up the debris from an aircraft crash. I was unaware of the crash and more focused on "where do I go once we land, will I be able to find my way, who will I meet?" all those questions that a new experience provokes.

We were given instructions to go to the end of the Midway complex, up several floors to the place called "the college." All of it, in that part of the complex was self-contained. We lived, slept, ate, studied, attended classes and got hands-on experience with the aircraft. This was our home for the next five weeks.

I had never been away from home and had never been away from my mother except the times I have described. I was homesick for all my friends, my mother and my boyfriend Jay. There were a few phone calls, back and forth and letters. Phone calls were not as frequent then as they are now because of money. I had almost none and would not get paid for over a month.

For the next five weeks I studied, went to classes, met new friends, learned safety measures for several aircraft, and got a new look.

Money was something I knew little about. I was not like all the other girls. I was not as sophisticated, not as fashionable, nor as worldly or wise in the social graces. I didn't know how to drink alcohol without choking on the taste or getting terribly sick. I wasn't sexually active either, so I was branded a "hick from the hills."

Ex-airline stewardesses who reached their 32nd birthdays staffed the college. There was a lot of paperwork that had to be completed. One of the requirements was that a potential stewardess had to sign a waiver stating that when the "novice" stewardess reached her thirty-second year, she would move out of the air. She usually went into a desk job or home as a housewife. If the airline, by chance, had an opening in the school or at the airport counter, a woman might be able to take a job in the company "off the line." Thirty two years old was considered too old to fly and by age thirty-two a woman was no longer considered pretty. No longer useful.

A potential stewardess was one who was accepted by the airline, but not confirmed until the five-week course was completed and passed along with the assurance that she still met the weight requirements.

Once the school, safety training and uniform fitting were completed, an assignment was made. The new assignees were usually sent to the colder locations because the warmer spots were bid on by those with seniority.

When I was told I that I would be going to Buffalo, New York, I was devastated. I would never see my parents again, never see Jay, my life was over. I wrote a long letter to Jacqueline "Jackie" Jackson, the director of the stewardess school. I told her a fabrication about how my aunt had paid for all of my expenses to attend stewardess college and that my parents were very poor. I explained that my aunt could travel with my parents by bus to see me in Texas; otherwise I wouldn't be able to see them until I was assigned a place that they could get to. It worked. My boyfriend Jay was stationed in Big Springs, Texas, and we would be able to be together.

Graduation day came and I was excited that I had completed the course. My parents were not able to come. My father had never flown.

"When it's your time it's your time," my mother told him. "God makes that decision."

"What if it is time for the pilot to die?" My father responded.

My parents did not have the money to come to Chicago but did send me a telegram. So did my friends and cohorts at work. I landed in Dallas, Texas at Love Field on April 21st, 1955. There were eight of us who decided to room together until we found a place to live. American Airlines (AA) had us stay at a hotel on Lemon Avenue.

It was more culture shock coming to Dallas than I was prepared for. The temperature was 90°, and that was different by 60° from the cold, slippery slush of Chicago. It was too hot, humid, and sweltering in Dallas. I had on wool clothes and no summer clothes with me. My mother had to send me other clothes. And while some may think that Texas is a Southern state, Texas is actually a place with its own culture. It is a state that was once a country and was not part of any other cultural region.

We checked into the hotel, and I thought I would have a few days to acclimate, and think over the last few days, which had been hectic. Fat chance! I was called to take out the first flight of our class. The next day I was to leave Dallas and then fly out of Amon Carter Field to Oakland, California. I would fly on a DC-7 with 56 passengers, and it would take six plus hours. I was horrified at the prospect of finally putting into action all that I had play-acted.

I'm not sure how many passengers were on my first flight out of Dallas, or if they enjoyed their trip but I sure had a blast. As we flew over the Grand Canyon I was so awed I forgot I was working.

After several days, eight of us found a small two-bedroom house close to Love Field. We thought a two-bedroom house would work for eight of us because seldom would all of us be home. After one month of nerves and misunderstandings, four of us moved into a more modernized apartment. The apartment had two bedrooms, but also had two bathrooms, so we took it. One roommate from Boston was given a puppy from her dad. The puppy was very frisky and very cute. The problem was that our roommate was never home to take care of him. She would lock the puppy in one of the bathrooms while she was gone, so we couldn't use it, which was not good with four women going in different direction at different times.

After one month of bedlam, I moved into an efficiency apartment on the corner of Cole and Lemmon Ave. I was still crazy for Jay as he was for me. Each weekend that I was not flying he would come to Dallas or I would go to Big Springs. We would talk and plan to get married, but whenever it was time to set the date, one of us was not ready. He would convince me to set a date and I would tell him, "Let's wait a year; let me fly and get it out of my system." The weekend that I was ready, he would ask me to let him finish his training and find out where we would be stationed. We went back and forth like that for several months. I continued to fly, model at Neiman's department story, and get adjusted to being away from my mother.

Jay graduated from pilot training and I went out to Big Springs to pin-on his wings. His parents and younger brother were there. Jay's daddy and family really liked me. Jay's daddy told him to grab me fast because he would never meet another girl as nice as I was. Jay told me what his dad had said and urged me to set the date.

We went back to my motel where Jay had reserved rooms for his folks and me. I was still a virgin and terribly afraid of getting pregnant. Jay was a very loving, mature and considerate man. He never used force or blackmail on me. He let me know in every way he wanted me but never said things like, "If you loved me you would." We were affectionate, but we didn't make love. I had decided I would fly a minimum of two years and a maximum of five. If I were not married I would lose my virginity at twenty-five. Bad girls were the ones who were going all the way when they were in high school or afterwards when they were not married. I surely was not a bad girl.

Jay was transferred to Washington state and I was tearful and lonely waiting for him. I worked as many trips as I lawfully could, went out with the gang and missed Jay.

A trip to San Francisco was scheduled with a girl I didn't know well, but we had some classes together and even worked a couple of flights together. We had worked a previous trip to San Francisco, which was a very popular run ending up with us having fun going out with a couple of dentists. She was a hit, although reserved, although some people thought she was cold. However, once she was around you and became more comfortable she was friendlier. We had a full load and with only two stewardesses, we were busy. We served cocktails before dinner. Sittings across from the gallery were two men. They each had had a drink or two and obviously had more before the flight. Finally we began to talk with them. They were both military, one was going on to Japan, the other was visiting family outside San Francisco. I told the other stewardesses we would accept their invitation to go out to dinner when we landed. But I wanted to go with the taller one since I was tall. She agreed and we continued the flight.

The boys were jovial, fun, flirty and looked acceptable. but there was no love at first sight for any of us; just four healthy, red-blooded, Americans kids. The flight ended uneventfully and with my ability to memorize all the passengers' names, I stood at the door saying good-bye while my co-host began picking up around the plane. Our admirers stood back, waiting for all the other passengers to deplane. I figured it was so they would have more freedom to ask us out and not be embarrassed if we turned them down. Little did they know we were going to make their day and go out with them.

The young man going on to Japan came off the plane first and said, "Miss Guest, thank you for wonderful trip. I will think of you while I am in Japan," and with that he went down the ramp.

I turned to the other man, thinking that of course, the other man, Lyle Burgess, would do the asking out, at least I hoped he would. He seemed a bit more sophisticated than the other man did. More debonair. After all he'd had several martinis which meant he was suave!

"Miss Guest, thank you for a wonderful trip. You are truly marvelous to say nothing of being a most beautiful woman. I shall spend my days and nights dreaming of you. Until we meet again, my dear, good-bye." And with that he sauntered down the ramp while I stood with my mouth open. No invitation, I was flabbergasted! This never happened to me. Most flights produced many invitations and we were usually saying, "no, no thank you." But this was a first!

I returned to Dallas, continued flying to San Francisco and took-up tennis. I was not a good player but a determined one and practiced when I could.

About two weeks after having my ego pushed into the bulkhead I had arrived in Dallas at 6:00 A.M. from a long flight. I was exhausted and all I could think of was bed. Thanks be to heaven, my roommate was out on a flight, so I had the apartment all to myself.

I fell into bed, asleep before my head hit the pillow. The phone rang again and again before I could rouse myself enough to answer it.

"Hello," I mumbled.

"Hello. Are you going to church this morning?"

"Will you leave me alone. Bob, I just got in from a hard flight, I'm tired and sleepy and don't call me again." I screamed at Bob as I slammed down the receiver. Bob lived two apartments down the hallway and was a good friend of ours, but sometimes a nuisance.

The ringing began again and I felt I was a prisoner of the phone. Finally, I grabbed it again and before I could use choice words, the voice said, "Please, Miss Guest, don't hang up and this isn't Bob. This is Lyle Burgess. Captain Lyle Burgess. Do you remember? Do you remember me?"

"I have never heard of you," I said, "and why are you bothering me?"

"Please, I apologize if I am bothering you. I just wanted to see if you would have dinner with me."

"Have dinner with you?" My voice was getting shriller and angrier. "I don't even know you. Wait a minute," I said as I was getting more awake. "How did you get my phone number?"

"Miss Guest, I was on your flight to San Francisco two weeks ago on October 15th. I was seated across the galley with another man. You were sweet enough to give me extra martinis. Do you remember now?"

"No," I yelled and slammed the phone down. I was steamed. How dare some skirt-chasing, booze guzzling, jerk call me.

One of the safety measures AA insisted on was for us not to give out our phone number or address. We were in the public eye, but we were protected.

When I received another phone call and when I answered, there was a pause before anyone answered.

"Miss Guest," a tentative voice asked, "Please don't hang up and I hope you are in a better mood. This is Lyle Burgess."

I was in a better mood since I had finally gotten some sleep but I was not pleased to have this man, whoever he was, calling me. "What do you want?" I asked.

"Will you have dinner with me?" Lyle asked.

"No, I can't," I lied. "My brother is in town and I must be with him."

"I'm disappointed," said Lyle "but I will call again."

My roommate was curious as to who this man was. I didn't date much, occasionally going out with Joe, Art, Gene-some of the old gang in the group, but no one steady, not since Jay was gone.

"He is some jerk who was on a S.F. trip and some how he got my phone number. I have no desire to go out with him now or ever, "I told her.

"Jan, don't forget. You have to eat," she said. We were eager to have dinner with our friends because we never had any money, and the cookies, peanut butter and coffee we existed on got old fast.

A few days later another phone call came from Lyle. I was out of excuses, missing Jay, and remembering my roommate's admonishment, I said yes to his invitation.

I was not excited about the date, more an endeavor I must get through. We went to Mario's, a well-known restaurant in Dallas. It was very nice old and elegant. Lyle had brought a Merlot wine as mixed drinks were not served in Dallas at that time. We ordered beef stroganoff, which I had never had and I had felt very lovely and grown-up. Lyle was a witty, urbane, complimentary, and an attentive date. I don't remember what we talked about. After all, this was just a one-shot deal as far as I was concerned.

Lyle did tell me how he got my phone number. He had a friend, Anne, who had sworn him to secrecy. She knew someone at headquarters who had access to the AA directory, so she gave him my number.

We said goodnight, but nothing about getting together again.

My roommate was home and asked how was it. I said, "I didn't impress him and he didn't impress me. But dinner was sensational."

Jay and I were still talking by phone and some letters, but I could feel that the distance was more than miles. Jay assured me that all was well, but my trust level was not high. Jay was charismatic, and all women found him irresistible. I felt he would succumb to the temptations out there, and I would be left alone.

Lyle continued to call me and expressed a desire to see me again. I was lukewarm; pining for Jay, I finally went out with Lyle. We talked about unimportant things. He was stationed at Carswell A.F.B. in Fort Worth, Texas, about 40 miles from Dallas. He wanted me to join him for a squadron party and meet his friends and the other crewmen.

That night when I got home again I thought, "no interest." We were not to be an "item" by any means. He still had not tried to kiss me and this was truly out of the ordinary. It was difficult for me to think a man was interested in me if he was not groping me. My knowledge about men was minimal. All I knew was that they yelled, slammed doors, and walked out. I didn't know they were introspective, sensitive, compassionate and respectful.

That night after Lyle left, I was so lonely for Jay. My roommate was out on a flight and I was alone, and all my other friends were working. So

I called Jay. It was then that I told Jay I was going to get married. I said that I was marrying a lawyer who was in the air force, who wanted to have a baby girl and name her Susan (Jay and I had talked about having a baby girl and naming hers Susan) and that this man was from Indiana. I went on and on like this. Lyle was unaware of any of this. We had talked, but not about personal things. I had no idea he had a college degree and one more year to go to get his law degree. I did not have any idea if he wanted to have a girl or name her Susan.

I was crying, talking, crying, all the while hoping Jay would talk me out of my *plans.*

But Jay was quiet and said "if you're happy."

I said, "I'm not happy. I'm miserable but this is what's going to happen."

I hung up, crying so hard that I thought I would explode. I had just told the man I thought I loved that I was going to marry another man. Was I crazy or what? I do not know where all this came from. All I knew was I hurt more than I can ever describe.

———•———

Lyle and I began to date more often. After our third date he did kiss me. He was not overly aggressive, but very affectionate. He was an old-fashioned gentleman. He believed women were women, men were men and was proud of it. I was certainly a product of my environment, and I was truly "the little woman." My job was second to his; I was important only if he thought I was. We were a couple.

We continued to go back and forth between Fort Worth and Dallas. More and more we were joining Lyle's friends. We were attending squadron functions, dining with other officer's and their wives.

Lyle's best friend and fellow crewmember was John; his wife's name was Jo. Lyle introduced me to them and their two daughters Marcia and Shelley. After Lyle and I were dating I would go to Fort Worth and stay over-night at John and Jo's house. Lyle owned a house a few blocks from them, but it was not *proper* for a nice young woman to stay at her boyfriend's house in 1950's.

We loved to dance and we were good at it. Many of our dates were at dinner-dances at the Officers' Club. I would stay over at John and Jo's then Sunday morning we would all go to church. I felt a sense of family when I was with them and their two little girls.

Lyle had two roommates, men who were also in the air force and single. They decorated the house completely in one afternoon, in about thirty minutes. It must have been after a pitcher or two of martinis since the décor was faux Danish modern and plastic accessories. But it was clear that Lyle was a responsible homeowner. I was impressed; I had never had a home. Even though this was a small two-bedroom wood frame, it was still a home. In the front yard was a lovely acacia tree with beautiful blooms. In the backyard next to the window of one of the bedrooms, was a bushy thing that I later learned was a fig tree that was filled with succulent, sweet figs.

Lyle was a navigator on a B-36 aircraft. His squadron, the 492nd, belonged to the Seventh Wing under the SAC commander Genera LeMay. Many times the SAC crews had to go on maneuvers. They were gone from their homes for days, weeks, even months at a time. And many times at a moment's notice they were called out with no time to say good-bye or do anything else. When they were in SAC they were on alert. The B-36 was a monstrous airplane and had been around for awhile. The missions that the men flew were potentially fatal. Those of us left at home did not understand how dangerous this was. At least I didn't, and if the other women did it was not discussed with me.

The glamour of the "fly boys" was not lost on me, nor was it new. I had spent four years working at a pilot training facility in Georgia and had exclusively dated airmen, so I knew the allure, the mystique, the romance of flying. When flying is in your blood it never gets out.

My mother wrote to me sometimes and occasionally we talked by phone. I went home after Jay was sent to Savannah, Georgia. and called him. I wasn't engaged but I wanted to see him. I don't know why I was playing such head games, except that I wanted him to play Sir Galahad and take me away on a white horse. We didn't get together, and I cried most of the time that I was at home.

———•———

Christmas was coming and I was scheduled to fly, so I asked my mother to come to Dallas. She agreed to take the bus to Nashville, Tennessee, and I arranged to pick her up as I came through Nashville from New York. I was excited because she would get to see me at work. I could get her a pass to fly and we could have a fun day together.

Lyle planned a special dinner party for my mother at a lovely restaurant. I had bought her a beautiful wool suit and she looked so pretty. She was smitten with Lyle and he was charmed by her. He was exceptionally charming and witty that night and we all enjoyed each other.

At one point Mother asked me to go to the ladies room with her. We were in the restroom, and she asked to me how I felt about Lyle. Lyle had left no doubt in her mind how he felt about me. I knew she thought that he was okay, but he wasn't Jay. She said, "Think seriously about Lyle. You will not meet a man like him again for a long time." She really liked him.

My roommate, Margie, and I were close and we frequently double-dated. Unfortunately she was dating a married crewman, but she was sure they would get married as soon as he got divorced. The oldest lie in the world was being perpetuated, but at the time we were naive. Christmas was rapidly approaching, and Margie and I decided to cook Christmas dinner. My brother Jack, his wife Dell and their three-year-old daughter, Jackie, were living in Dallas. Margie and I thought it would be great fun to cook a traditional holiday dinner and invite all the people we knew who could not go home for the holidays. We would make our own family and our own festivities.

Neither of us had ever cooked, and we knew no more than how to boil a cup of water and make peanut butter and jelly sandwiches. The morning of our inaugural dinner we went out in the morning to play tennis. We decided we would cook when we got back. The guests were scheduled to come over around noon. My brother and his family were there at 12:30 p. m.. Jack said he was hungry and couldn't wait for dinner. When he looked in the kitchen, which wasn't hard to do since we lived in an efficiency and saw no preparation going on for dinner he became a little terse. "Where is dinner?" he groused.

Margie and I looked at each other and decided we had better get busy. We got the frozen turkey out of the refrigerator and that's when

Jack said he and his family would see us later. They were too hungry to wait until midnight! Lyle and Margie's boyfriend Simon stayed the entire afternoon, offering a bit of advice here and there, and we finally had dinner at eleven o'clock. Lyle said he couldn't tell what was what. The gravy was the consistency of mashed potatoes and the mashed potatoes was the consistency of the gravy.

Lyle's relationship with me was on again, off again. I was the one who would decide we shouldn't see each other anymore and for no particular reason. He would wait a week or so and call and I would see him. This went on for months. On Valentine's Day, 1956, he gave me an engagement ring. He was leaving for French Morocco and would be gone for two weeks to a month, but he promised me that he would write. I floated around for a day, looking at my ring, enjoying the attention from the other girls, until I hit the brick wall. There sitting in the cockpit was the most gorgeous man I had seen since Jay. Lyle was distinguished and elegant but not handsome. This pilot was knockdown, to-die-for, handsome. We were no sooner airborne than he called me up front. He wanted to know where I was from. "Moultrie, Georgia," I replied. "No kidding," he said, "I am from Xenia, Ohio."

Later he announced over the loudspeaker that "Miss Guest, your stewardess, is from Moultrie, Georgia, and I, Captain Whatsis, is from Xenia, Ohio." You could see people turning to each other with the question mark, "Where?"

He also was at the root of my breaking my engagement with Lyle. How could I look at him and think the way I thought and still be engaged? There was no hanky-panky. Some of the girls were having sex, but I don't think they were in the majority at the time. Most of us were too afraid of getting pregnant to chance it. But there was some old-fashioned kissing and a little touching, Enough that I didn't think I should be engaged. Wasn't I committing adultery thinking the way I was about another man?

Lyle and I were married eight months after we met on June 17th, 1956.

Jan, age 36, at tea ceremony in Japan.

Right: Jan, age 3.

Below: Jan, 16.
High School
Graduate.

Below right: Jan,
Senior Prom.

Below left: Jan, 22.
American Airlines
Stewardess.

*Right: Jan, age 24,
with Lyle and Paul
at home.*

*Left: Age 35.
Jan and Lennie
at Officers' Club.*

*Below: Age 49.
Jan and Pat, wedding day.*

*Left: Jan, age 35,
modeling in Japan.*

Above: Jan, age 63, in Panama.

Right: Jan, age 66, on top of Macchu Pichu, Peru.

Below: Jan, age 67, in China.

Below: Jan, age 69, in Costa Rica.

Thursday morning in Columbus, Mississippi, bounced on the horizon like an impatient child. "Time to get up!" It was October 15th, 1959, a perfect day, cool and sunny with blue skies.

Melissa Montgomery Burgess was two months ten weeks old, and Lyle Paul Burgess was two-and-three-quarters years old. They were both up, awaiting the day and all the excitement and surprises that were to be theirs.

I was up with the little ones, getting Paul's breakfast and fixing a bottle for Missi. Lyle came into the kitchen, kissed me good morning, and roughhoused with Paul.

"Remember that I go out on the chrome dome tonight?" Lyle said.

"Yes, I do," I replied. "Are you excited? You have waited for this. I know you were disappointed last month when you were bumped."

Lyle nodded yes. He was a pilot and a navigator. He was going on the first flight for the B-52 to stay in the air for twenty-four hours. The B-52 was to refuel while airborne, and Lyle would fly along with two student navigators, with Lyle as their instructor. There would be five more on the B-52; an eight member crew.

Lyle was getting his fishing tackle and his gear together. He'd figured that he'd get rid of some stress by going out in the woods to hunt and fish. Whenever he went out he always came back with some food for our table.

The morning passed with the daily chores of two babies to tend to and housework. Lunchtime came and Lyle came home to have lunch, then a nap before it was time for him to report to operations for his flight.

My mother was visiting so I invited Millie, our across the street neighbor, over for lunch. She and Mamma enjoyed each other's company. I fixed rarebit on toast and quarter lettuce with Russian dressing. We talked and laughed our way through lunch. We talked about the flight since Millie's husband, Milt, would be the lead pilot. It was a history making moment.

It was time for Lyle to leave for operations. We were standing in the bedroom. He had kissed the baby goodbye. He put his arms around me, pulled me in close, and said, "What more can any man want? I have you, we have our boy and now we have our girl. I went fishing and hunting this morning and I'm getting ready to take a ride in the greatest aircraft—I ask you, what more could any man want?" He was grinning as he kissed me.

Paul and I took Lyle to operations. He kissed us good-bye and said he would see us the next day.

We went back to the quarters. I was sewing a dress for our leave. We were going to Wisconsin in two weeks to visit Lyle's aunt and uncle. Lyle was going to teach me to use a bow and arrow. I had just shampooed my hair and was cutting out the dress on the dining room table. Mamma and I had fed the babies, bathed them and put them to bed. We were watching Groucho Marx on TV when the back doorbell rang. I said to my mother as I went to the door, "I'll bet it's Millie." I opened the door and there stood the colonel's wife, Kay who was married to Lyle's aircraft commander. With Kay was the chaplain. I didn't know him, but I knew he was a Catholic chaplain.

Kay said, "Can we come in, Jan?" I stood to one side, embarrassed that my hair was still wet, my dining room untidy with the patterns and material scattered about.

The chaplain and Kay came in. My mother stood up and as she did I looked at her and said, "It hasn't been five years yet." She screamed. Kay and the chaplain said a plane had gone down, but they didn't have a lot of information.

My Mother said, "Jan's in shock."

No, I wasn't in shock. I was remembering something I had told my Mother just before Lyle and I were married. I told her that I didn't think the marriage would last more than five years. She said, "If you are thinking divorce, we can stop everything now." "No," I told her, "that's not it. I feel that one of us will not be around longer than that."

She said, "Oh, you just have bride's jitters. You'll be okay." But now she looked to be in shock herself.

There had been a midair collision when the KC-135 came in to refuel the B-52. All four crewmen on the KC-135 were instantly killed by a flying gas station. There were some men who got out of the B-52, but they didn't know who.

I can't explain the feeling; it was instant numbness, along with heightened awareness. Confusion. Fear.

It would be twenty-four hours before I would know if Lyle were dead or alive.

The quarters filled up with people. It was a little after 9:00 P.M. I paced. As new people came in, I asked them what they knew. No one had definite information, just that a huge explosion had happened around six-thirty. Some of the other crews flying missions had seen the explosion. In my small, two-bedroom, government quarters there was lots of activity. Everyone wanted to help, but there was nothing to do. Just wait.

Several times I felt someone at my elbow saying, "Take this, Jan, it will relax you. Scotch and water." "No," I said, "I don't want a drink. I want to stay alert in case I need to go to Lyle." After several attempts to get me to have a drink, I said, "Please. I don't want a drink. I only drink with Lyle once in awhile when we're having fun. I'm not having fun now."

A nurse whom I had seen at the hospital, but didn't know came over to me and said, "I want you to take this. It will relax you." She was holding a black pill in her hand.

I again said, "No, I don't want anything. I want to stay alert in case I can help Lyle."

I couldn't sit down. I paced. I asked the chaplain if the church was open. He said, "We can open it." I wanted to go to the church and pray. The chaplain, Kay and I went.

I walked inside the church, the hush was as quiet as snow falling. I went up to the rail and knelt. I started praying out loud, "God, please help me. I'm scared. I don't know if Lyle is dead or alive. If he's alive, please, God let me get to him and help him. If he's not alive, God, help me with these children. Guide me and direct me in their raising. Help me to know what to say to them and what not to say. I don't think I can do this, God, not by myself. I ask you to help me. Amen."

Kay was crying. The young chaplain, was misty-eyed. We went back to the quarters. More people were there. I stayed outside for fresh air. No one wanted me to talk about Lyle. When I would say something they would shush me, "Don't think about it," they would say.

I couldn't swallow. I couldn't drink water; my throat wouldn't work. All night I sat and waited, washed over in fear.

Millie's husband Milt had ejected. We got that news and that the co-pilot had ejected. Then we heard two more had gotten out. Hope abounded. If they got out, maybe the others had.

Through the night I paced. The morning came and no news. Mid-morning I walked out to the carport and Paul was in his daddy's combat boots. All I could see was Paul's head and shoulders. The boots engulfed him. He was so cute. And to think in a few hours his life was to be devastated.

One of the guys was standing in the carport looking at the children. He said, "Jan, you're young, you're pretty, and you'll marry somebody. This will be behind you." I looked at him in horror. What was he saying? Marriage? I was married. If Lyle was dead, I would never marry again. Did he know what he was saying? I just went back in the house, feeling worse than ever.

At six that evening an officer came to tell me Lyle was dead. They had to identify him by his dental records because there was nothing else left of him. He was burned to extinction.

There were two student navigators, and Lyle was seated in a jump seat behind them. When the alarm sounded the student navigators were to eject, making a hole for Lyle to go through. The student navigators froze at the controls and Lyle was trapped.

Paul, Melissa, Mamma and I were to get out of quarters immediately. Lyle's brother drove down to Mississippi from Indiana with a cousin who would drive my car back to Indiana where Lyle was to be buried. Mother, the children and I would fly.

Sunday, before we were to leave, I attended a memorial for the fallen men. I was the only wife left. As I walked back into my quarters after the service, I passed out. Just crumpled to the ground like an autumn leaf. They rushed me to the hospital, IV'ed me, and I slept for twenty-four hours. I had nothing to eat or drink for three days.

We were in Indiana for a week. Lyle was buried in his family's plot. With full military honors. When the bugler started playing *Taps*, I felt my very heart being split apart. The firing of the rifles just about did me in. But hearing *Taps*, those haunting, heartbreakingly woeful sounds. I dissolved. I wept. I felt my life was over. I had died. I wanted to die. How could I go on without Lyle?

Sitting at Lyle's gravesite where there was nothing of Lyle, since he had burned up when the B-52 and KC135 blew up, I couldn't keep my mind from wandering. I knew I was in the underbelly of fear. How could I manage with two babies, my mother and myself to support? I couldn't go back to flying. You were not allowed to fly if you were married or if you had children. And during that period of time you didn't have babies without being married! I could do office work, but what kind of job? Work was hard to get, and being a secretary was one of the few jobs that women could do. Teach school, nurse or office work. That pretty much covered the job opportunities.

6

After Lyle

How would we live? The government had us out of quarters and off base in just days. We went to Indiana where Lyle was from and for the burial.

The government gave me the compensatory $3,000, that was given to all widows. It was six-months pay and that was to get us on our feet. Lyle and I had about $500 in the bank and that was all the money I had. I was driving a 1953, red, Lincoln convertible that needed a lot of engine work and replacements for the bald tires.

My mother was coming to stay with me since she had no place to stay. Daddy had died and she was alone. She would live with the children and me. Needless to say, this had not been thought out. But we were both staggering, blinded by need.

My biggest decision was where to live. Columbus, Mississippi, where we were based was not a choice. Going back to Moultrie, Georgia was definitely out. So Fort Worth, Texas, where I had lived off and on for four years, seemed the right choice. My mother, two-and-a-half year-old Paul, two-and-a-half months Melissa and I chugged our way out there. After flat tires, engine problems, unbelievable tiredness and suffocating sorrow we arrived in Fort Worth.

It was agreed that my mother would take care of the children and I would find a house. We immediately moved into a very sparse apartment while I began looking for a house. Never in my wildest dreams did I think I could buy a house. The one Lyle had bought before we married and the one we lived in after we married was sold. A few weeks after we arrived in Fort Worth, I received an insurance check for $10,000. Lyle and I had talked about taking out some insurance on him, but I tossed it off saying we were too young and didn't need to spend our money that way. He took out the policy just before he was killed. Premonition? My goal was to buy a house, bring up my children, and send them to the best school I could afford and save my money so I would always be able to provide for them. I was so scared. Lyle had been such a force and strength in my life. He was witty and cultivated. He could drink liquor and still be warm, funny and civil. I didn't know how I could manage without him. Not just his financial support, but in my emotional life too. He would encourage me to talk and open up to him and although I didn't know how, I attempted to do so. Now, my strength and support were gone. He had encouraged me to enroll at TCU when Paul was six months old. I was twenty-three, married and attending classes with 18-year-old freshmen.

I was scared. Of everything. Of life. Of my mother. Of my children. Not scared of them, but for them and that I would not know how to guide them and direct them. I was getting criticized from every turn. I could do no right, or so it seemed to me. If I corrected Paul, my mother would get mad at me. If my mother thought Paul needed correcting and I didn't she was mad at me. I felt mired in a microcosm of mishmash, and no way out. How could I take care of two babies; an aging mother, who was all of forty-seven-years-old; work; earn money; and make all the decisions a family needed to live? I was back to that feeling of not wanting to live, but how could I leave my babies? There had to be a solution, but it was not in my grasp.

I had a desire to own my own home. While my mother took care of my babies, I found a house in a section of Fort Worth called Ridglea Hills.

A two bedroom, red-brick, two-bath, living/dining room, den, kitchen with breakfast area and two car garage, nice yard, and it was heavenly.

I was scared beyond words, but I put pen to paper and figured out I could buy the house, $16,000, and have it paid off in time for Paul and Melissa to start college. And my mother would always have a permanent home, which she had never had before. I bought the house and spent the next six weeks painting the brown interior walls white, taking down the hideous cabbage rose wallpaper in the kitchenette area and repainted it. I sewed drapes and put them up in the living room, painted louvered blinds and put them up in the kitchen. I had never done any of these domestic chores before. Of the $13,000 I had, I spent $1,500 at closing on the house and $1,500 getting a refrigerator, stove washer and dryer. And un-heard of at that time for us "little people" my one luxury, I bought a king-size bed.

After six weeks of twelve-hour days getting the house ready, Mamma, the children and I moved in. We resumed a routine, Mamma taking care of the house and babies; me working. I wasn't highly qualified for any-thing, but I got a job in a mattress factory (where the king-size bed was made) and enrolled in nine hours of college. I worked eight hours, came home to eat and see my babies, then three nights a week I was off to college. I was totally overwhelmed but had no idea that I was doing so much. I felt completely inadequate because I wasn't doing more.

My mother was not happy, and I didn't know how to make her happy. When I got home from work she had a list of things Paul had or had not done. And she wanted him punished immediately. I hadn't seen him all day and I wanted to love him and play with him, but if I did that my mother would be furious and not speak to me for days. I had a glimpse of what my father and others of his generation must have felt. Our mother told us kids if we didn't behave "Wait 'til your Daddy comes home." That would put the fear in us. And so I would get home and need to go into the disciplinarian role. Yet when I did portion out that discipline, my mother was not happy with the way I did it. Such friction!

My mother totally depended on me. I had to buy her everything she needed or wanted. Including her cigarettes. I received $400 per month and I paid the mortgage, car payment, bought food and clothes for four and anything else we needed. There was a great store-plan back then, lay-a-way. A few dollars down would hold most any merchandise. A few dollars each month until it was paid. Most of the baby's clothes and Paul's clothes were bought this way. Although I was in perpetual fear about everything, I was very responsible. I paid all of my bills, worked hard, studied for my classes, kept my family together and was slowly dying inside.

I had no social life; who had time or energy? When I was not at work or in school, I was giving my mother a break from the children. My mother helped me tremendously. I don't know how I would have managed and yet deep down in my soul I knew we were not succeeding. We did not have a healthy environment for any of us. My mother was very controlling and was most upset if I didn't agree with her. When she was unhappy she would be silent and would not talk to me. She would tell Paul, "Tell your mama to pass me the salt," or any other normal request. It was very uncomfortable, but eventually she would start talking to me.

The most difficult times for me were in the late afternoon and early evenings. That was the time Lyle used to come home. It was as if the children recognized his absence. They would cry and whine; nothing satisfied them. I took them and my mother in the car and we'd drive around until they were sleepy. At times we would stop at Lone Star Drive-In on Camp Bowie, where Mamma and I had a beer and French-fried onion rings while the children ate ice cream. We didn't do this often because of money, but Mamma enjoyed a beer occasionally, and it was my way of showing her people could have alcohol and still be happy with no fighting.

More and more I was having problems with Paul. He didn't like his baby sister and didn't understand why we had her and not his dad. He would say "send that Missi Melissa Gumery (he couldn't say her middle name Montgomery) Burgess back and give me my dad." He missed his dad. They were very close while Lyle was alive, and now Paul was acting out. Mother doted on Missi, and Missi seemed to gurgle and coo her way into everyone's heart.

I felt torn, not enough time for work, school, mothering and all the things I expected myself to do. I felt since Paul was walking and talking I should give him the most attention and my mother could take care of the baby. I realize now that the baby needed more of my attention and love than I physically gave to her and that only added to my feelings of guilt.

The children were sick a lot, and I had to give up more than one job. In 1960, it was difficult to get help even if I could afford it, which I couldn't. Mother was a good cook and would have a hot meal prepared in the evening. I wanted to talk about Lyle, but from the beginning of his death I was told not to talk about him. If I started crying, thinking about him and missing him, I was told to "stop crying;" time I got over that; you're stronger than that; it is a weakness to show your grief; keep a stiff upper lip; and "smile so no one knows what's inside." I bought the whole ticket and I didn't even know how to grieve even if I had been allowed to. The times I had tried to talk to Lyle about my father I would tear up but never bawl the way I wanted to. Nor could I talk about my dad. When I finally wrote about Sopchoppy I was fifty-five years old. I had never told anyone about that time.

Many times I would sun myself out on the patio and let the tears quietly run down my face, pretending it was sweat in case my mother walked outside and saw me. She told me once that when I was a toddler, no one knew I was crying unless they looked at my face. I didn't make a sound. Guess I learned very early to keep my grief and sadness to myself.

We slipped and skidded our way in this fashion for about ten months. I was at the breaking point, and Mamma was close to one herself. We were getting on each other's nerves. My mother had no outside activities and resented my going to work. She felt in charge of the house and I resented this. We had no idea how to resolve conflict. All she knew was to yell, scream, slam the door and pout with her silence. Since I had grown up on this from her and my dad, I knew no other way either.

Paul had gotten into some mischief, as three-year-old boys are prone to do and my mother demanded I "whip him." I refused and with sudden, looming awareness I knew somebody was going to get it and it wasn't going to be Paul. Maybe. I felt that I was going to kill my mother, Paul or myself, if not all three. This was serious and I knew I needed help. I called Carswell Air Force Base Hospital and made an appointment with a doctor.

The next morning I dressed as if I was going to the White House for luncheon. Hair and make-up done to perfection, high heel shoes, mink stole, gloves. No one, especially a doctor, was going to see anything but perfection. As I sat waiting for my name to be called I wondered what I would tell the doctor. That I wanted to kill someone? Hardly. Doctors were next to God in my opinion in those days, and I knew he would definitely know what to do.

I went into his office and sat down and without looking up at me he asked, "What's the trouble, Mrs. Burgess?" He was looking at my chart and finally looked over at me. He did a quick up and down scan and said, "You don't look like anything is wrong."

"There really isn't," I muttered.

He said, "All your vital signs look normal. Do you have any complaints?"

I, again, said, "No, not really."

He began asking a few questions. "Who do you live with?"

"My ten-month-old daughter, my three-year-old son and my mother," I answered.

"Where is your husband?" the doctor asked.

"He was killed," I choked back the tears.

That doctor's fist hit his desk so hard it bounced.

"Why didn't you tell me that in the beginning?" he yelled.

"I didn't know it was important," I said and began to bawl. I cried and cried and he let me. When I could catch my breath, he asked how long it had been since I had cried. I said I hadn't.

From there he devised a plan for me to get on with my life. I told him all the things I was doing, working, taking nine college hours, babies, house, mother, and sickness. He told me the first thing I was to do was to get rid of my mother and take total responsibility of my children and myself. I'm sure I just stared at him. Had he any idea what it was like to tell my mother anything? Let alone to leave? What planet did he live on?

I listened to him and as fearful as I was at the prospect of telling my mother any of the things the doctor and I talked about, it all made sense. Maybe with my mother living somewhere else, we could have a better relationship, and my children wouldn't be exposed to such chaos.

I went home with a bucket of worms crawling in my belly, but also with a feeling of hope. There was a workable solution to this, and we would all be better off for it. My mother needed a life as much as I did. She deserved some fun and a life other than taking care of my children, although I hadn't given any thought to how I would manage without her. I knew once she heard what the doctor recommended, she would understand and we could work things out.

I went home and Mamma immediately asked what the doctor said and I told her we would talk later. There was something I needed to do for the children. Several more times she asked and each time I made an excuse and told her I would tell her later. Finally, I knew I could no longer hold off telling her, so I suggested we go to Lone Star Drive-In and have a beer. The children were excited to get ice cream. We sat at the drive-in, and she asked again what the doctor had said. I could tell by her voice that she was getting concerned, maybe I had a fatal disease, or was completely crazy and would be locked up. And she would be left with the children! What a fate.

As gently as I knew how I told her the complete story, what I said what the doctor said and what the doctor recommended. When I said, "He thinks it would be better if you lived on your own and the children and I live on our own," she just stared at me. I felt the fury building long before I heard anything.

She stared at me and said, "You are the most selfish person in the world. All you think of is yourself. You think you are so mistreated just because Lyle was killed. Well let me tell you. You will pay for this. Take me home, oh, excuse me to *your* home!"

"Mom, please, let's talk this through. I don't think I'm mistreated because Lyle was killed, but the doctor said I have experienced a tragedy and I need time to heal. Please don't be mad at me." I was crying.

She never looked at me. Just stared out the window. We went home, to my house, and for the next two weeks she did not speak a word to me.

One of the Kiwi's (ex-American Airlines stewardess) I knew had a son Paul's age. He was enrolled in an exclusive preschool. The students were there by invitation only and old Fort Worth monied families sent their children there. The teacher was ancient, but renowned for her abilities in child rearing. My friend talked to Mrs. Whoosis and she agreed to take Paul. Paul had had his third birthday three months after his dad was killed. I took Paul to school three mornings a week. Missi and I would take him at 8:00 A.M. and pick him up at 11:30 A.M. With his grandmother now gone, I felt this school would be a big help. My job had been seasonal, and I was not working so his school was priority. Missi and I loved taking him and she knew when it was time to pick him up. She was almost a year old and loved her "Pa-Pa." She couldn't say Paul, but he knew who Pa-Pa was. He still wasn't crazy about her but he tolerated her some of the time. She adored him.

We were at the school to pick Paul up one day when out came a teacher, with Paul in tow. She was practically dragging him she was walking so fast. I was scared. I could tell she was mad and I was worried over what my child had done. My mother would often tell me if I were a better mother my children would be better children. But I didn't know how to be better. I thought I was doing pretty well but her criticism always hurt.

The teacher pushed Paul in the car and demanded, "Show your Mama your arm!"

Paul held up his little arm and there were pink teeth marks on it. I gasped and was ready to do something to the child who bit my son when she said, "Settle down. I bit him."

"You? You bit my son? What's wrong with you?" I was now yelling.

"He bit the back of the child in front of him. I bit him so he would know how it felt. That's how I train children not to bite. He won't bite any more." With that, she turned and went back into the school.

That's how she trained children? I was so intimidated and unsure of my own ability that I thought, "Maybe she's right.' I didn't like it but didn't know what else to do. I needed help and who was I, too dumb, stupid and ugly to contradict the most powerful teacher in Fort Worth?

I had made friends with the neighbors across the street. Their house sat on a small, lovely little lake, and I would sometimes take the children over to feed the ducks. My neighbors had no children and doted on Paul and Missi. After we were there about a year, they had a baby boy.

Paul loved the lake and was growing into an independent little boy.

Too independent! He would go out to play in the yard and I could see him from the window. He was a good little boy, very manly and usually would listen to me and mind me. But he began to wander off, go out of the yard, and disappear. I would go out on the back stoop and call him. Or look on the patio. No Paul. I would call and call, start looking in the side yard, no Paul. With an infant it was difficult to juggle both a baby and a disappearing toddler. I was very fearful he had gone across the street and fallen into the lake. Finally, he would come trudging home. I would scold him, tell him how dangerous it was to go out of the yard and that he would be punished if he did it again.

I would be so upset at having to be so stern with him that I would cry into my pillow after he and the baby were asleep. The next morning he was gone again! I spanked him, put him in his room and grounded him. He cried himself to sleep. I cried myself to sleep. The next morning he was up and gone before I knew he was out of bed. I found him, really spanked him, went across the street to my neighbor and told her I just knew I had ruined Paul for life. She gave me two aspirin and said he would be fine.

The next morning he was gone again. I called the lumber company and asked them to bring me enough lumber to build a fence. They asked me how much lumber. I said, "enough to build a fence in my backyard so I can keep my little three-year-old boy in the yard!"

The man laughed and said, "Calm down, Mom, we'll get things worked out." He told me how to measure and what I needed for supplies and he could deliver them that day.

I built a fence even though I never even put an erector set together let alone a fence. I put a gate in and a lock on the gate. At last. I would feel secure with Paul playing in the yard where there was enough room for him to play. The next morning after I built the fence, I got up and looked in on the baby and looked at Paul's bed and he was gone!

Drastic measures, more than just a mere fence, had to be implemented. I had no idea what to do. Spanking him, harsh talk, keeping him in his room, none of these things were working.

I was standing in the kitchen when I saw him coming up the little hill in the backyard and I had an idea. I would scare him into submission. As he walked in the back door, I was holding the receiver of the wall telephone.

I said, "Oh, that's okay, Mrs. Bracher, Paul is coming home now. I'll tell him what you said and I do hope it works." I hung up the phone, which had only a dial tone, and turned to Paul.

"Paul," I said, "that was the lady from the orphanage. Do you know what an orphanage is?"

"No, Mommy," he said.

"Well, an orphanage is a place where little boys have to go when they don't mind their mommies. Like you do. You keep leaving the house and I can't find you. I have explained how dangerous that is for a little boy."

"And a little girl, Mommy?" he asked.

"Yes, and a little girl. You must stay in the house until I tell you it's okay to go out and you must stay in the yard. Do you understand me?"

"Yes, Mommy, I understand," that sweet, angelic son of mine said while putting his arms up to hug me.

I totally melted, hugged him, kissed him on the cheek, breathed a sigh of relief that we had finally resolved a very difficult problem. Sleep would be forthcoming soon and I didn't have to wake up to my son's empty bed.

We had a lovely, quiet evening, the three of us, playing. Paul said his prayers and I tucked the children in. Peace at last. No crying myself to sleep, secure in the knowledge that my son was safe and would not leave the house without my knowledge.

Gone! As soon as I woke up I knew instinctively he was gone. And it was so early. The baby was still asleep. I was on the verge of madness. I was so angry. So angry at my runaway son; so angry at my lot in life; so angry at the air force; and where the hell was Lyle when I needed him?

I went to the back door, after making sure Missi was still asleep and her crib sides locked in place. I was going out the back door when I saw Paul coming up the hill. I reached over to the wall phone and as Paul came in the door I said, "Yes, Mrs. Bracher, it breaks my heart to give up my little boy but I don't know what else to do."

Before I could get all that said, Paul was shrieking, "No, Mommy, no, please, I won't leave home again. Please, I promise," sobbing hard tears. "Please don't make me go away," he cried, hugging me around the knees.

"Mrs. Bracher, can you hold on just a moment?" I asked. I turned to Paul and said, "Paul, I can't keep doing this. You aren't minding me and I don't know what else to do." I was blinking fast to keep from bawling. My heart was breaking. I loved this little boy more than life itself yet I was whipped. I was lower than low, and felt like a complete failure as a mother and as a human being.

"Please, Mommy, I will never leave home again, I promise," he was crying.

"Well, Paul, if you think you can stick to your word and that means you do what you say, then I'm willing to give you another chance."

He went to his room to play and I went to my room to stop my flood of tears.

With much trepidation, I awoke the next morning. My son was asleep in his bed, and he didn't leave his own yard again.

We were adjusting to my mother being gone. Missi missed her a lot because my mother did everything for her. Missi was a sweet little girl. The black hair that she was born with had come out and she was completely bald. Soon white blonde little tufts came in and she eventually had a full head of hair. She was learning to talk, and she was especially excited about "Santa Closets and his Raincoats." She would stand at night and look at the "gars and guy" (stars and sky) and she would take her "hoos and hocks" off so her feet could feel the grass. Missi was a charming, loving little girl and any man was a candidate for her father.

I heard her talking early one morning at the kitchen door that went into the garage. She was putting her words together pretty well, but they were still coming out a bit garbled. "You be daddy," she was saying.

I knew the screen door was locked, but I didn't remember if I had closed the garage door. I rushed to the kitchen door to hear Missi say, "And you sleep in Mommy's bed."

Who could she be talking to, I wondered?

"And," she continued, "you be my daddy." She was so excited.

Standing at my back door was the garbage man, tobacco juice running down his chin, his toothless grin as big and bright as the rising sun.

I thanked him for his trouble and for picking up the garbage, picked up my daughter and cuddled her with my heavy heart. She was missing a daddy figure because everywhere we went she gravitated towards the men.

We were driving home from the Officers' Club pool one evening when Missi threw her arms around my neck, almost strangling me. This was in the days long before car seats or seat belts were used. They weren't even in most cars in the 1960s.

She said, "Mommy, Mommy, I know what we do. I got good idid"

"What is your idid, baby?" I asked, smiling at Paul who knew idid was idea.

"We can go to Sears Roebuck and order a daddy. I see them in the book. Let's do that, Mommy, let's do that!" The more excited she got the stronger she strangled.

Explaining to my children why they didn't have a daddy and where he was stretched all of my knowledge and emotions. How to explain the un-explainable to a child?

We three were experiencing a lot of changes. The children were grow-ing and learning and so was I. None of it was easy. But most of it left an impression.

After my mother left I thought I would feel grown up, the adult mother of two children. Yet I found myself angry, angry at everything, most espe-cially the U.S. government. We were in the midst of the Cuban Missile debacle. Lyle had told me, just before his death, to keep the trunk of the car filled with bottled water, and at any sign of trouble to start driving west as far as I could go. Carswell Air Force Base was possibly one of the bases the missiles were directed to hit. I had canned goods and water and many nights I worried what would happen to my children if we were attacked. Sleep had been difficult to come by most all of my life. And now was certainly no exception. The children would waken in the night or they would be sick or I just could not sleep.

One night I was reading quite late, the children were asleep. I heard a different sound. I continued reading and heard the sound again. My ears were perked up high, "what was that sound?" I listened intensely and, yep, there it was again. A slide across a patio with a leather soled shoe. Someone was on my patio! I just knew it. I was never a fearful person, but I was aware and alert. Especially when it came to my children.

Again there was that sound, a slide across concrete with leather. I put my reading light out quickly and looked out the bedroom window. Black expanse stared back at me. I went into the bathroom adjoining my bedroom and looked out the window. From that angle I could see the beginning of a moon, but no man on the patio skipping. I was perplexed and began to get scared. I needed to get to my children's bedroom. I stood very still, contemplating what to do. As I started towards the bedroom, I was shocked into stillness. There! Again, there was that noise. I was in such fright by this time that every muscle was tense. I could hardly move, again I heard the scrape. Now it was over my head. I looked up with such fear, not knowing what to expect, was there a man in my ceiling? Was he going to hurt us? Hurt me? Hurt my children? Again there was a scrape and I decided to face my demons and what other peril might be waiting.

I had no weapon other than my sheer determination that nothing would happen to my children or me. I looked up to the ceiling and saw a moth that looked as big as a B-52. I reached up, grabbed that moth and stomped it, kicked it, punched it, and called it more dirty words than I even knew.

I vowed that night I would never be afraid again. I could not afford to be because I was too immobilized when I was in that kind of fear. Besides, the next morning I could hardly move from having been so stiff all over.

Life continued, the children growing. Paul's tonsils were flaring up every time the wind changed. The doctor said it was necessary to have them taken out. I had such difficulty giving permission for this surgery, yet the severity of Paul's illness could not continue. We scheduled the operation, and I took Paul out to the hospital. I was scared but tried to assure Paul that his health would be much better after the operation. I had left Missi at the base nursery and stayed in the waiting room during Paul's surgery. I was alone. It seemed as if a lifetime had passed before Paul was taken to ICU. He was not awake when I went in to see him. He was mumbling. He looked so tiny, so alone, and as I took his little hand and leaned down to kiss his forehead I heard him say, "Daddy."

My heart sank. Even in his drug induced sleep he wanted his dad. I picked up his progress chart the nurse had left on his bed table, and every few minutes the entries were "calling for Daddy," "saying Daddy." His dad had been dead for a couple of years, yet he was still calling for him.

Since I was the only parent my children had and there were no relatives for 1,000 miles I tried to teach them as much as I could. I took them to museums, art galleries, and the theater (we had to leave in a hurry a few times because of boredom or temper tantrums, or the usual child's fussy behavior) and I taught them how to swim, although I couldn't swim very well myself. I remember when I was about five, my dad threw me in the river and told me I would automatically swim. I almost automatically drowned. Years later telling this story to a friend, she said "Jan, he wasn't trying to teach you to swim!" Not funny.

The children and I would go out to the pool at Carswell Air Force Base and swim. They would play in the kiddie pool, and occasionally I would ask another mother to watch the children while I got into the big pool for a quick cool off. Paul was not afraid of the water, but he was more hesitant to try new things. Missi was fearless in the water, and although two-and-a-half years younger she was more aggressive. Paul began to follow her lead and soon they were both swimming. Missi was two and a half and insisted on going in the big pool. I would stand in the shallower end and bounce her up and down. There were two low diving boards and one high dive. I didn't dive at all, but could side-stroke and float, which was the extent of my swimming. Missi decided she had to go up the high dive. She had watched people go up and jump in the water. She was hooked. I stood at the base of the high dive and watched her little white-blonde hair, tiny legs, climbing up five billion feet in the air. She was so small she had to climb by pulling her body up on the next step, one leg at a time until her whole body was on the step, then she repeated the process until she was at the top. She was being watched and she knew it. She would stand on the diving board, look all around to make sure everyone was watching, spot me in the water, then jump. I would hold on to the bar of the steps, stretch my arm as far as it would go and grab her as she came up. She would pop-up, eyes open, her lips like a little fish and dog paddle to me. We did this over and over and she loved the attention.

She was learning different words and sounds, but she had difficulty with the ess sound. Shoes and socks came out "whose and hocks," stars and sky came out "gars and guy." She also loved the idea of Santa Closets and his raincoats instead of Santa Claus and his reindeer.

I taught the children the proper words for body parts and was amused to hear her talking one-day. I followed the sound and realized she was sitting on the toilet talking to herself. She was rehearsing the words I had taught her. She was saying "Un huh, mommies, little girls and Missi have baginas and daddies, little boys and Paul have peanuts."

Paul came rushing in one day from playing in the yard and wanted to know if we had a shovel. Since we did our own yard work, I thought maybe he was going to "play" work in the yard. I told him we didn't, but we could probably borrow one from our neighbor. "But why do you want one, Paul?" I asked.

"I just want to dig up my daddy and talk to him. I just want to talk to him for a few minutes. Don't worry, Mom, I will put him back when I finish." I was crushed with the pain.

Missi and I were visiting my friend Martha one day. She had a little girl named Beth, who was the same age as Missi. Martha's husband came home while we were there. Leonard rushed in, picked up Beth, threw her in the air and kissed her. He was so happy to see her. I glanced over at Missi and saw such longing on her face; it matched the longing in my heart. I grabbed her and left. My children were missing so much. I hated the air force. The very same organization Lyle had loved I hated because it had taken him away from me.

I had several jobs such as a receptionist at a country club and an accounts payable clerk for a local television station during the next few years after Lyle was killed. Each job went by the wayside when I had to miss time because one of the children got sick. One job was at a state medical facility, but that job ended when the doctor told me he would set up an apartment where he would come to meet me without anyone knowing. Including his wife, I assume.

I also flew part time for American Flyers, a charter airline. Flying for the AM Flyers was the only way I could get a vacation. What I made in pay went towards paying someone to stay with the children. I went to Canada a few times with hunting and fishing clubs' expeditions. I realized that I needed the time away once in a while.

About a year after Lyle's death I began to see a major who had been stationed at Columbus Air Force Base, Mississippi. Earl's wife had committed suicide and I had sent him a note of condolence saying, 'if I can help in any way let me know.' Not long after that he arranged to see me. He was the only man, other than Lyle, whom I had made love with and I felt considerable guilt. Good girls didn't, and good girls certainly didn't enjoy making love. So what was wrong with me? I was doing *it* with Earl and except for the guilt I enjoyed it. Earl began coming to Fort Worth on weekends. I envisioned us having a family. Earl had a twelve- year-old son from a previous marriage, and I said bring him along so we could all get to know each other. I couldn't imagine not marrying him, since we had been intimate. We had done *it*, so we must be in love and in love meant marriage. Earl would drive to Fort Worth from CAFB, spend the weekend and drive back. Most of his time was on the road, but we were in love and any sacrifice was worth it. Earl adored Missi as did most people. Paul was growing out of the toddler stage and into the little-boy-awkward stage. To me he was a sweetheart, but I could tell he was not as appealing to Earl as Missi was. But I knew he would learn to love Paul. It would just take a little time.

Earl was coming for the weekend and bringing his son. I was excited. We would put our families together as a start to a beautiful future. 'How much happier could I be?' I wondered. He arrived, but without his son. "What's wrong?" I asked "Is your son sick?"

Earl said, "No, he isn't sick. He came into the room where I was waiting for him and he was sucking his thumb. I told him no son of mine would suck his thumb, so I left him home."

I was devastated. He had told me he hadn't seen his son in several months and then he turned away from him because the boy was sucking his thumb? I was dumbfounded. Besides, Paul sucked his thumb. That same weekend Paul awoke from his nap and sleepily he wandered into the den where Earl sat half reclined on the sofa. Paul climbed up on Earl's chest and put his thumb in his mouth, continuing to wake up. Earl picked him up and put him on the floor. I was standing in the kitchen where I could see them and the expression on Paul's face crushed me. If Earl could walk out on his own son, what would he do to mine? I was still confused about Earl and still thinking we *had* to get married because we were having sex.

87

I had many doubts until our chaplain came to see me. "Jan," he said, "there are many people concerned about you. We all love you and fear that you don't know some truths about Earl. Did you know he's been married?"

"Oh yes," I answered, "I knew Jackie a little, his wife who committed suicide and he was also married to his son's mother." I felt I knew Earl. The chaplain had no reason to worry.

"Yes," he said, "those two times plus two more. You would be his fifth wife if you marry him. Many of us don't think he's good enough for you. You deserve better."

I felt deflated. And disillusioned. How could Earl overlook telling me about two marriages? Goodbye, Earl.

There were others, but not many.

7

Gino and Nick

And then there was Gino. He loved me, and he loved my kids even though he had four kids of his own. I said he was divorced; he wasn't, but that little fact came out after I was a goner and so were my kids, really gone.

We were gorgeous together. He was tall and handsome, very mannerly and considerate and very married. I was crazy about him. I met him at the Air Force Officers' Club. During the years of my widowhood I had had a couple of relationships, but nothing that made me feel the way I did with Gino. When we were together we danced, took my children to the park, had backyard barbecues and enjoyed life. Life was good.

I still had to manage the guilt of it, liking a man, liking intimacy, liking the feeling of being a whole family. Then on top of the guilt, other guilt; the guilt of his marriage. He told the age-old stories, how his wife didn't understand him, how they got married only because his wife got pregnant, how they were too young to know any better.

Then Gino was transferred; he was moved to a base in Indiana. That was somewhat of an inconvenience, but we managed to be together when he came down on flying missions.

Being a product of my time and environment and wanting so much to please the man I loved, I cooked and cleaned until the house was spic-and-span, everything perfect for him.

I wanted my children perfect, spotless and free of whining. I prayed they would be on their best behavior.

Then my mother came to visit. After several months of her absence and silence, I gave into my guilt and called her. I was crying, "Please talk to me, Mamma." I flew her in at my expense and picked her up at the airport. I got her favorite foods, smoked turkey, different cheeses and fancy crackers and her favorite brand of vodka. She loved being back with us and played with the kids until way past their bedtimes.

Great, I thought, we could sit together, have some food and drinks and talk. We could be like grown-ups with each other. As I was making our drinks and putting a tray out on the coffee table, she was in the bathroom, so I thought.

Suddenly I heard her yelling from the hallway, "You whore," she yelled over and over.

I moved into the hallway and saw her standing in front of the open hall closet. In her hand was a bag from the dry cleaners with a current tag on it.

"Mamma, please quiet down, you're going to wake up the children."

She just looked at me, anger steaming out of her pores. "He lives here, doesn't he?"

"Who? What are you talking about?" Then I saw the tuxedo as she pulled it off the closet rod.

"This," she said, "This doesn't belong to you. You have a man living here. You slut! You are just a whore," she screamed.

"Mamma, please settle down, that belongs to a musician friend of mine. He was playing here and then had to go to another gig. He didn't have time to pick it up, so he asked me if I would get it and hold it for him until he got back into town. That's all there is to it. No one lives here but me and my two children."

When she lived with us for those ten months, whenever she got angry with me over anything she would threaten to take my children away from me. She accused me of being an unfit mother. That seed planted into my consciousness a long time ago was if I transgressed in some way I would lose my children. I was so insecure. Back then it wasn't easy to be a single parent; it wasn't accepted. I had no one to discuss parenting skills with, no one to help me make decisions, no one to pat me on the back when times got rough, no one to help me keep a sense of balance or assure me I was a good mother.

Here my mother and I were again, at odds. She glared at me and said, "I can still take these children away from you."

It never dawned on me that she could not do that. She was a widow, with no money, no home, no transportation, and all that escaped me because I believed her.

———•———

Gino came down. Again I had made things perfect for him, the wife he should have with a spotless house and good food. Gino arrived on a lovely Saturday afternoon. The children were happy to see him. He was equally attentive to Paul and Melissa. He had two boys and two girls and knew how to play with children and could connect with them. He was perfection. My mother was still at the house, and I knew she would have a fit when I returned with him. To my surprise she didn't, but she was very chilly. A couple of hours later when I came back to the living room from the kitchen, my mother and Gino were gone. They were in the bedroom with the door closed. I didn't think much about it. I reasoned that Gino was probably telling my mother when we were going to get married and that he was just waiting for the divorce papers to be finalized.

They came out of the room and I noticed that my mother was smiling, but Gino was looking a bit grim. He told me he had to call operations and check in. When he came back into the room he said he had to leave, the air force was calling him back to Indiana. I was terribly disappointed, but I understood that the air force came first. I drove him back to the base and on the way, he began accusing me of seeing other men. I was stunned. I thought he knew that I believed we had a *virtual marriage*, which meant I believed I was married to him. There was no other man.

91

There had been numerous rumors that I had heard about Gino that he had been seen with another woman (not his wife) in Indiana. But I didn't say anything to him about it because I trusted him. I just knew he wanted to get his divorce, have us get married and we would live happily ever after. Why, all of a sudden, was he pulling the jealousy routine on me? We had always been friendly with other people, maybe even a bit flirty; we were both friendly, social, outgoing people. But now, as we drove to the base, he continued to berate me about seeing other men.

I was very sad when he left and upset that he would even suspect me of seeing someone else. This had not come up before in our relationship. Why now? I went back home and found my mother contently playing with the kids. My mother could change her mood so fast that I had a hard time keeping up with her. She had been so angry and accusatory about the tuxedo, cold as ice when Gino arrived, and was now calm and serene. After the kids were put to bed that evening, she asked me how Gino was when he left. I said he was okay, then suddenly a small, wiggly-worm started in my stomach. Something familiar, something nasty was trying to hatch inside of me. I didn't want it to because I didn't know just what this feeling was about, this feeling of worms gnawing away at my guts, but it was familiar.

"Well," she said, "I had a talk with him."

I remembered they had been in the bedroom talking, the hot, gnawing worms multiplied, a nasty taste formed in my mouth. "What did you talk about?" I could hardly get the words out.

"Oh, just things," she said, smiling.

The worms were moving faster, producing the bile that I was tasting. "Did you tell him I was seeing other men?" The words spewed out of my mouth with such venom, that the words escaped with them. All that remained inside of me was the steel cold knowledge of betrayal. My mother knew that I knew. She gave me a hard look and walked out of the room. I turned into my old self, the little girl following behind her pleading "Why? Why?"

I cried myself to sleep. The same way I did seven years earlier when Nick, a cadet I dated, suddenly told me out of the blue that he couldn't see me anymore. I cried with the same intensity as that day. The day he told me he hoped I would understand; that he loved me, would always love me, but could not date me anymore. I cried for days. If I could just understand why all of a sudden, with no warning, he couldn't date me anymore. After weeks of crying and wondering, I finally decided he liked another woman. When he sent me flowers, I broke the stems off the flowers, put them back in the box and sent them back to him. He could not play with my affections and get away with it. I would show him!

————•————

Nick's mother used to send me homemade candy. His family was from Armenia, and the candy had an unusual taste to us. My mother was upset that I was dating a foreigner with dark skin, and said the family probably didn't even speak English. Nick had been born in the United States and had graduated from primary flight school in Mississippi. My girlfriend's boy friend was also stationed in Mississippi. He knew Nick and told her about him. This was his story about Nick.

Nick arrived at advanced flight school on probation; he was weak in some areas of the program, but was determined and was willing to do whatever was necessary to stay in flight school. While he was in flight school, he was dating a girl whom he really loved and wanted to marry her; her name was Jan. Then one day his flight instructor, Henry pulled him aside and said, "You have a choice to make, if you want to stay in flight school and graduate, you have to stop seeing the girl you're dating. You have to stop seeing Jan. If you continue dating Miss Guest, you are washed out."

Nick loved flying; he had come up through the ranks, worked his way into flight school with out the benefit of ROTC. He was a smart, dedicated student, and followed all the rules. Trying not to be insubordinate, he said, "May I ask, Sir, why I must stop seeing Miss Guest?"

"Because, her mother does not want you dating her."

Nick did not know the rest of the story, but my girlfriend's boyfriend did. Henry wanted to date me himself. My mother agreed to fix us up, but only if Nick was out of the picture.

My mother liked Henry, but I did not. Henry was from Texas. He wore cowboy boots and hat when he was not in uniform. He was a stereotypical "redneck," definitely not my type.

After Nick stopped seeing me, Henry would come by my office to ask me out, but I would tell him no. He would come by my house and my mother would invite him in, feed him, pretend he and I had a relationship. It seems that everyone in the neighborhood knew about the charade but me. I would learn of my mother's meddling after I was married to Lyle, had two children and was widowed. I was still grieving from my loss of Lyle. When my girlfriend told me about Nick and how distraught he was about what my mother and Henry had done and how the despair had caused him to flunk out of flight school. I was shocked. Some said he had had a nervous breakdown. I cried and cried for days.

Now, as with Gino, I was crying again. I called him to find out what had happened, and he told me the whole conversation he had had with my mother. Just like Nick, my mother had come between me and the man I loved. Ironically, I later found out that the rumors about Gino and another woman in Indiana were true. So was my mother in trying to protect me, proving offense is the best defense, or was she trying to keep me from love?

I am not bitter. I do appreciate the compassion Gino showed my children. For example, one time I took the kids to visit their aunt and uncle. Gino was stationed near where they lived. He went with us to Lyle's gravesite; I was wiped out and so emotional I couldn't even talk. He took Paul and Missi and talked to them about their dad and how great he was. His kindness helped.

I felt so depressed and so betrayed by both my mother and Gino. It seemed to me that he was dying to see me all the time. My mother, through her own experiences, could read people very well and she recognized Gino's insecurity, so she pounced on him like a panther.

She successfully broke us up, but in thinking about what she did with Nick, I did not know how to feel about her motives. I was wary of letting her know I had a boyfriend, if I ever did have one again.

8

Lennie

I met Lennie in June of 1963. Our recollection of when we met differs. He remembered that he met me at a house party on Lake Worth the year before. I remember the party but do not remember meeting him until June 1963. Friends introduced us at the Officer's Club. He was known by all the single ladies as a "good catch." I thought he was too old for me, but he was a nice man. I began to see him at the Officer's swimming pool in the afternoons when I would take the children out for a swim. He had two children and his daughter and I became friends. I was leaving the pool one day when he asked me again to go out. I had refused him on several occasions thinking that he was just too old for me. He was thirteen years older.

Again, I was prepared to say I couldn't go when he said, "If you don't go out with me the next time I ask you I will not ask again."

I was so flippant and flirty, I said, "Oh sure you will."

He said, "No I will not," and that was that.

I went home and was getting supper ready for the children when the phone rang. It was Lennie. My hair was wet from swimming, the children needed to be fed, bathed and put to bed. But he kept to his word. I was to go out that night or he would never ask me out again. For some reason I believed him. Quickly I pulled my hair back and fastened a red flower over the bun. I put on a white lace sheath, called the babysitter and went out with him.

We went to a private club and had some drinks. We talked about how we never wanted to get married again. His wife had died two years before from a brain tumor and my Lyle had been killed four years before. I recognized that he was a wounded soul also. We did not go out again for a month because he was out of town taking his children to visit their aunt. My children and I went to visit my mother in Georgia. When we both returned to Fort Worth we began to see each other every day. Three months later we were married. I was surprised. I didn't think I would ever marry again. Yet somehow this seemed right. We were in love, his children needed a mother and my children needed a father. We were meant for each other and God was smiling down on me again.

We were married on a Friday afternoon at the Congregational Church in Fort Worth, Texas. We had a small reception at my house and drove to Dallas for our honeymoon. The four children were staying with friends.

My two children and I had been living in the house in Ridglea that I bought right after Lyle was killed. Now we were to move to Carswell Air Force Base because Lennie had to be close to his job. He was a B-58 pilot and they were frequently called out on missions.

We moved my things into his quarters and assumed life as a family. His son was fourteen and his daughter was twelve. My two were six and four. I was now the wife of a lieutenant colonel., and I had the responsibilities of an officer's wife.

Lennie stood six feet tall. He was a distinguished looking, witty, a gentleman to the core. And he was dedicated, no married, to the air force. He was a career officer and his first duty was to the military. I should have known that, but I was in love and thought love would cure all.

One of the first things I was to learn was how to drink alcohol. I learned to drink a little with Lyle. I did not like the taste of liquor, but I got used to it. Lyle drank scotch and water and so did I. We sometimes drank wine, but that took some getting used to. When Lennie and I went to Dallas on our honeymoon, the air force and navy were playing football in the Cotton Bowl. Lennie's good friends, Buster and Kay were in town for the game. Buster was a two-star general. When we got to the hotel, it was 11:00 A.M., but Buster and Kay were already drinking gin over ice. It was early for me and my stomach was not settled. Buster started fixing drinks and handed one to me. I said, "Oh, no, thanks, I do not want anything to drink."

Kay said, "Jan, if you are going to be an officer's wife you must learn how to drink."

I dutifully took the drink, pretending to sip along with them. I would encounter this attitude many times throughout my life.

Alcohol had encroached on my life ever since I was a small child. It affected my father and my brother. It would continue to be an invisible partner for most of my adult life.

———•———

Lennie died on a Tuesday night, January 21ˢᵗ, 1970.

He was on an inspection tour with General Steloff from headquarters in San Antonio. We had been in Misawa, Japan for six months. Lennie was commander of a wing in Misawa with the other bases in Japan, Korea and the other Pacific stations. The tour had begun on a Sunday afternoon. I took Lennie to base ops to catch his flight. On the way I suddenly asked if he wanted to extend our marriage another week. We had played that game since we married. I told him I thought I would keep him around because he was fun. He reached out and took my hand in his and said, "What more could any man want? I love you, we have the kids and now I'm starting the greatest job there is." Cold chills ran up and down my back. The exact same words Lyle had said ten years before. I squeezed his hand and changed the subject.

Lennie was to be gone for a week, coming back on Friday. We were sponsoring a party for the inspection staff and Lennie's team. What Lennie didn't know but was to be announced at the party, was that he was being promoted to brigadier general. That was his dream. He had been promoted to full colonel just three years before. He was an air force star and he would soon be wearing one.

I kissed Lennie good-bye and went back to the quarters. On Monday night he called and we talked about the arrangements for the party.

Tuesday was a cold, sunny day. January in northern Japan is very cold. It had snowed during the night, but the day warmed up and melted the snow. I had duties during the day, and several schoolteachers called me and asked me out to dinner with them. They were a fun group, liked Lennie and my children. We went skiing up in the Japanese Alps, had dinner and danced at the Officers (O) Club. They would come over to the quarters for a glass of wine and talk.

Tuesday night we went into Misawa to a Japanese restaurant. I was restless. I told the girls I needed to finish eating and go home. They wanted me to go to the O Club with them for an after dinner drink, but I felt compelled to go home.

The kids were in bed, as was Mitsuko. Mitsuko lived with us and helped around the house and watched the children when Lennie and I went out.

It had started snowing again. Soft, silent flakes floated down from the sky. The moon was brilliant, almost as bright as day.

I sat in the living room listening to Herb Alpert and the Tijuana Brass. I couldn't go to bed. I tried but was restless. I paced back and forth from the bedroom to the living room. I looked out the window and watched the snow. I looked through the blinds and saw a chaplain and Lennie's assistant. Before they could knock I had the door open.

"Was it a plane crash?" I asked.

"What?" The chaplain said.

"Jan, let us come in," said Lennie's assistant.

They came in. No one knew what to say. I said "Lennie's dead, isn't he?"

The chaplain took my arm and led me over to the sofa. "Len had a heart attack and at 10:15 p.m. was pronounced dead. One of the staff members was sharing a room with Len. They had gone to bed just a little earlier after having dinner and drinks at the O Club. The staff member heard a noise. It was Lennie. He thought Len was reaching for the light to turn it on, maybe to go to the bathroom. Then he heard a thud. He turned on the light and found Len lying on the floor. He quickly ran next door where he knew a doctor was staying and had the doctor come in. Maybe a minute or two passed. Then the doctor pronounced him dead."

The chaplain took a deep breath. The assistant said, "Jan, he didn't feel a thing. It was instant."

I sat in numbness. My brain cells were depleted. My body was as still as the night.

As I sat there, I remembered something I said to Alice, a friend of mine, on the tenth hole of the Kadena golf course about eight months before. I said, "Alice, I'm worried about Lennie. He's under such stress and he has been since we went to the Pentagon. I'm afraid he's going to have a heart attack." Alice just looked at me. Air Force wives didn't talk about their problems, certainly not about their husbands.

Yet, as I sat there I remembered our physicals three months before. We went down to Tokyo to Tatachikawa AFB and were in the hospital three days taking a numerous range of tests. It was the most thorough physical I have ever had in my life. I didn't believe Lennie had had a heart attack. He was six feet tall and still weighed the same as he had during his high school football-playing days, 175 pounds. Although we drank, ate a lot of red meat and (Lennie) smoked, we also played golf, danced and were very active.

I sat there dazed, confused, wondering how this could happen to me again. Ten years between husbands' deaths. How could I tell my children their dad was gone? The two older children had lost their mother just eight years before. My two had lost their dad ten years before, and Lorri, the youngest, was only five.

I felt someone standing by me. I looked up and realized our living quarters had filled with people.

"Take this, Jan. It will help." Again, same as when Lyle was killed, someone was giving me a scotch and water.

"No," I murmured, "I don't want a drink."

It was cold. The heaters were working as fast as they could, but the cold air was seeping in through the window and doors, and people kept opening the door to enter the house.

The air force was in full gear. They would pack us up and have us out in a day. Where did I want to go? Where should they send the household goods? Where would we go? I tried to think, but my brain was anesthetized. Asleep. Dead. Not functioning.

"Jan, we must make arrangements. You've got to tell us what you want," the assistant was saying.

"Yes, yes, I know," I said. "Just let me think."

Where would I take our children? The oldest boy was at Texas A&M. How could I again tell my children, our children their dad was dead? People were asking me if I wanted to wake up the children.

"No," I told them. "What can they do at midnight? Let them sleep."

The Chaplain was asking where I wanted the body sent. 'Body? That's no body, that's my husband.'

"I'll tell you what I want," I said.

"What?" They asked.

"I want an autopsy."

"An autopsy? Now Jan, You're just upset. You know the air force doesn't do autopsies."

They were placating me and I knew it. There was no way Lennie had had a heart attack. He was too healthy, too young. He was forty-nine. I was thirty-six. I was twenty-six when Lyle was killed. Something had happened to Lennie, but not a heart attack. He had one of the highest security clearances given in the air force. All those times we had tried to go to Hong Kong and we were not allowed because if he or we had been kidnapped, he knew too much. Once, I tried to go without him but was not allowed. I knew I seemed paranoid, but something was wrong.

"I want an autopsy," I insisted.

They looked at each other. I noticed Dr. Baker had come in. "No," I said. "No shots, no pills. Don't try to knock me out. I've had that done once, and I won't allow it again."

About that time, all hell broke loose. The house was shaking, dishes were rattling, and the chandelier in the dining room was rocking back and forth. Hell was surely here. My husband dead, my children fatherless, where was I to go?

I saw two little figures race across the hallway. I jumped up and ran down the hall. Scooping up Lorri and Missi, I put them back in the bed. They were running to Mommy and Daddy's bed. I kissed them and murmured, "I love you." They were soon sound asleep, totally unaware that an earthquake had just hit and that their dad was dead.

I walked back down the hall stopping in Cappy's room. Cappy was sixteen and had her hair rolled in six ounce orange juice cans. She opened her eyes, and said, "Mommy, what a terrible way to wake up." She held her arms out and I knelt down beside her bed and hugged her. Did she know about Dad? Did she feel his death? Her grandmother told me the night Cappy's mother died that Cappy ran screaming into her bed. They realized later that it was at the exact time her mother had died.

I kissed her and walked into Paul's room. Paul, almost thirteen, was up-side down in his bed. I turned him around, covered him up, kissed him on the forehead, and returned to the living room.

The rest of the night was spent in planning sessions. The first order was for us to get off base. Get out of Misawa. For a second or two, I considered staying in Misawa. Moving off base into the town, putting the children in Japanese schools and resuming life. Was I crazy? I spoke a smattering of Japanese, and the children only spoke a few words. Lorri was more fluent than any of us, because she had had a Japanese nanny since she was three. But how would we live? I knew I would get some kind of pension but how much? So many decisions to be made immediately, no time to day-dream about where the children would thrive the best or where we might live. Just get out of quarters and off base now!

The night passed with murmured voices, coffee perking, whispers and questions. I let the children sleep until their regular time to get up for school. Paul was up first, and I told him his dad had passed, dropped dead of a heart attack. His eyes got misty, and he walked back in to his room. Cappy came out next and I told her. I held her as she cried. The two little girls came into the living room to see what all of the ruckus was about.

I took Lorri in my lap and sat Missi down next to me. I told them their Dad had died during the night. Missi put her head inside my arm, burying her head in my side. Lorri said, "What do you mean, Daddy's not coming home?" It was all I could do not to fall apart.

Paul and Cappy came back in the living room dressed for school. I said, "You don't have to go to school. You know it will be all over the base that your dad has died."

Missi spoke up and said, "No, Mom, we have to go to school. "We have to be there for our friends."

"They will be sad too," Paul said.

"Yeah, we have to go see about our friends and make sure they're all right," Cappy said.

I was so proud of my children for their compassion towards others.

Some way we managed to get through the next few days. Sunday a memorial service all over the Pacific was held at the same time. Saturday night Bill and Diane and our friends came by the quarters. When they started to leave, Bill said he would be working the next day.

After the memorial service, the usher came and got me and my family and escorted us outside. It was a gray day and the sky was bleak. Suddenly bursting through the clouds were four F-16's, one missing, signifying the missing man. Bill was the lead pilot. I now understood why he said that he would be working.

As we stood watching the missing-man formation, I was emotionless. I remembered saying to the children, "We will remember Daddy as a strong soldier and we will remain strong. We will not cry." Many years later, I apologized to my children for saying that, but in that day and time, emotions were not displayed. Accolades were plentiful for my show of strength. I was held forth as a remarkable woman for my strength and stamina. Inside, I was a wailing, raging wounded animal. I was scared. I was struck dumb with the impact of being left with five children. And yet I functioned. I consoled the many who came to offer their condolences. I made arrangements for Lennie's burial at Arlington National Cemetery.

The autopsy came back, and Dr. Baker told me that Lennie's main aorta was completely closed, and that within five years, he would've been in a wheelchair. I rationalized that Lennie would rather be dead than be incapacitated. Yet, 'just to have had his presence would have been a blessing,' I thought.

"Why God," I asked. "Why has this happened again to me? Why must my children grow up without a father?" I felt that God had turned his back on me. I felt alone and frightened.

I tried to pray. I went to church, talked with the chaplain, read the Bible, but I couldn't find peace. Fear was my prevailing emotion. Deep inside I trusted that God would be with me through the dark hours, but consciously I was riddled with doubt and fear.

We were packed and ready to go, but as irony played a big part in my life, nature came in with a roar. The soft, fresh snow turned into a blizzard. No airplanes were going in or out of Misawa. We were stuck. For ten days we were in limbo.

———•———

We moved back to Fort Worth, Texas. We resumed our lives as best we could. Our standard of living dropped seventy-five percent, since our income was gone. My mother offered to come and stay with us, but I felt, from past experience that it would be better if the children and I continued on our own as a family.

I started college on my fortieth birthday. Finally my dream of getting a college education was coming true. But college was not the only thing on my horizon.

9

Roy Again

The call came late at night, as unpleasant news often comes. My mother was crying. Her words were jumbled up, like she had a mouthful of grits, but still talking, all the while mushing grits and swallowing.

"Mamma, Mamma, please slow down. I can't understand you! Are you okay? What's happened?" I kept interrupting her gumming her grits.

She still had her teeth. She belied her seventy-one years. She looked much younger and had more energy than people ten years her junior. She still did nursing work at the hospital, mowed her lawn, kept up her house and baked cakes that were a treasure to receive. It was now the 1970s, but time seemed to stand still for her.

"It's Roy." I finally understood her.

"It's Roy," had been said, or so it seemed, all my life. "It's Roy" always meant bad news. "Roy is in prison; Roy has been stabbed and is not expected to live; Roy's beating up on me, come stop him."

All these things I had heard over the years. When we three, Roy, Jack, and I were in school, we would hear things like, "It's Roy. He's been expelled; he's beaten up on a boy," or "he tried to mess around with the teacher's daughter."

"It's Roy," my mother said again.

I sighed. I hated the way I felt, but I was weary of Roy. Why can't my mother call me up and say, "Jan, I'm so proud of you." Of anything. It didn't have to be something big or important, just anything. To tell me once she was proud. "What's Roy done now, Mom?" I asked.

"He's dead."

I could hear her catching her breath. The mushing and swallowing had stopped. There was a dead silence. No breathing. No swallowing.

"Mamma, are you there?" I thought she had hung up, but I had not heard a click. 'Maybe she's passed out,' I thought. "Mamma! Listen to me. Roy has been killing himself since he was born. Before he was born. You remember telling me how Daddy beat you up so badly when you were six months pregnant with Roy and how you feared the baby might be dead? You remember that, Mamma? Roy has been dying all his life!" I was practically shouting.

"Jan Baby, listen," my mother pleaded. She hadn't called me "Jan Baby" since I was twelve when I asked them not to call me that anymore. "Jan Baby, Roy is dead. Listen to me." She was softly crying now. No outburst, just a quiet resignation. A silent acceptance. "He's dead. I need you to come home. I need you to be here. Will you do that?"

I held the phone in a death grip. 'Here we go again,' I thought. No consideration of my time, my family, what I was doing, nothing, just, "come home." Like so many times before, I would drop everything, my job, my children, whatever was going on in my life, and go. "Yes, Mamma, I will come. I have to call the airlines and see what flights are available. I have to see if someone will look out for Lorri, but I will be there. I'll be home just as quickly as I can." Mentally I was already checking off the things that I needed to do before I left.

I was living in Dallas, Texas, with my youngest child, sixteen-year-old Lorri. Thank God for calm, peaceful, introspective Lorri. She was a joy to be around, and we seemed to have our life worked out. She was in school, still dancing with a ballet company and didn't seem to go through the teenage angst. I was a probation officer for Dallas County Adult

Probation. I had a very difficult boss and dreaded being off from work.

I made reservations, talked with Lorri and made her promise me that she would not touch the car and told her that our friend Sherri would be there if she needed anything. Lorri had received a hardship driver's license because of my long and often late hours. But I didn't want her to drive when I wasn't home.

I arrived in Atlanta in time to make my flight to Moultrie. There is an old saying, "When you die and go to heaven or hell, you must change planes in Atlanta!" And it's certainly true if you are going to the South.

A friend of my mother's met me at the airport. It was early Friday morning. My mother was worn out and distraught. She cried as she began to tell me what had happened the night before.

Roy had been on a rampage for a day or so. My mother had heard of his latest escapades, his escape from prison or whatever, as she often did: through the grapevine. Moultrie is a small town, and my mother had lived there for many years. There was some relief for her this time because the carrying-ons about Roy were not on the front page of the newspaper, as had happened before.

Roy, for many years, had fought Demon Rum (and other libations) and various drugs and narcotics. Nothing had changed. He was strung out of his mind, enraged. At what or at who was anyone's guess, including his.

At dusk she heard banging at the front door. She was in bed with the only light coming from the TV. She had worked hard at the hospital all day and came home to a bath, a cup of soup, then bed and TV.

When the banging started she thought maybe it was Roscoe, a neighbor who sometimes also got in the way of Demon Rum. He would comb the neighborhood looking for Wanda, his wife, and all the neighbors would hide out to avoid him. My mother waited, hoping it was Roscoe and he would leave. She had to work the next day, so she needed her rest, and watching TV helped her go to sleep. It was part of her routine. She got up every morning at five, even the mornings she didn't go to work.

Up at five, fix instant coffee, sit at the table drinking her sugar and creamed instant coffee and smoking a cigarette. Two cups of coffee, a cigarette and off to the bathroom. Anything to change the routine made her irregular and grumpy. So she stuck with her routine.

She said the banging didn't stop and joining the banging was a voice. Her son's voice.

"Mother, God damn it, open up. I know you're in there. Open up, damn it!" Roy was shouting.

Mother always worried, "What would people think?" and she hated "having linen aired. You don't air your dirty linen," she always said. She quietly and slowly got up, still hoping the banging would stop and Roy would leave. No one could reason with Roy when he was strung out.

"What do you want, Roy?" she asked.

"Open up this damned door," Roy yelled.

Mother quietly said, "Roy, I am in bed. I have to work in the morning. Please leave."

Roy screamed out some expletives.

Mother again was pleading with him. "Roy, hush, go on, now, go on. I need to sleep."

Roy was banging on the door as if he couldn't see or hear Mother. It was as if his own demons were running rampant in his head.

Finally, mother said, "Roy, leave now or I will call the police."

Roy just stood looking at her, cursed her some more, threatened her and said he would be back.

After he left, Mother was so upset. She tried to resume her TV watching, but couldn't put her mind to anything but Roy. She was and had been for years heartsick over her first born. He had made a shambles of his life. He had been married five times and had numerous live-in and live-out girlfriends. And fathered four boys that she knew of. Such a messed-up life. And yet she was partial to him. Maybe because he was so messed up. The old saying, "the wheel that squeals loudest gets the grease," applied with Roy.

Mother later told me she was restless, she couldn't settle down and even though she knew she needed to get to sleep, she couldn't even get back into bed. About 8:30 p. m. there was a soft knock on her door. She heard a voice, patient, calm call out, "Miz. Eloise, it's Billy Don. I need to talk with you."

With trepidation my mother opened the door and said, "Billy Don, it's about Roy, isn't it?"

107

"Yessum, it is. I best come in for a spell, Miz. Eloise." Billy Don came in and holding his hat in his hand, he said, "Miz Eloise, Roy's been killed. A bunch of niggers kilt him." He caught Mother as she tried to sit on the sofa.

She just sat and looked at him. "No, that can't be. He was just here. Twenty, thirty minutes ago. It can't be him." Now she was crying, crying with the realization of what had happened. Had she sent Roy to his grave? Had she sent Roy away from her house because her patience with his drinking and drugs and his anger had reached her wits ends? That she was too tired to hear him out? Was she the cause of his death? Questions whirled around inside her head.

"Is he in the hospital, Billy Don? Is that where they took him?" She was reliving the other times when she was on duty at the hospital and was called to come to emergency. Always it was Roy. Once, cut from one side to the other, perforating a kidney sliced almost in half. He survived to go on to many more cuts, slices and dices. Always one-step away from death. One more time outdistancing, outrunning, one more time, slipping away from death.

"No'em, they took him to Carl's. They ain't no more to be done for him 'cept what Carl can do. Don't you worry, Miz Eloise, you got friends in this town and your friends will take care of things, including them that kilt him." Billy Don was working up a steam. Billy Don was the "typical" Southern sheriff, including a big belly and wrap-around-reflective sunglasses

Mother said "They took Roy to Carl's? That means there is no hope for his recovery? He wasn't taken to hospital? He's dead?" Mother was crying, taking in the fact that her first born, always difficult, forever charming child was no longer alive. In a strange, sad way, there was a bit of relief. Relief that there would be no more headlines in the newspaper, no more midnight calls of rambling incoherence. No more calls or letters from prison. Also there would be no more times of cooking his favorite meal, sitting down and enjoying the food and the conversation. No more seeing the few times when her son would be sober, coherent and affectionate. No more of anything. Mother sat taking it all in.

Inactivity was unknown to Mother. She was decisive and action oriented. What to do? "I must call Jan. And I'll call Jack," she said, getting a move on.

Some of the townspeople and neighbors were already arriving. Mother was well thought of in her town. She had lived there for over thirty years. In the next couple of days there would be enough food brought in to feed all of us for days. My kids especially loved the varieties of cakes and other desserts that showed up at family funerals.

I arrived mid-morning, after mother called me. Of course, I was tired, no sleep, anxious, worried about my family, worried about how my mother was going to take this.

After I got some of the details from Mother and we decided on the time for the service, she wanted to go to the funeral home. Carl, the undertaker, had told her to come at any time. I didn't want to go, but gave in to her insistence; but I held my ground when she insisted I go in and see him. I did not want to see him. The police had told us how his head had been bashed in by bricks. Five young black men had surrounded Roy when he left mother's house and drove to "Nigger Town," and parked his yellow Cadillac in the middle of the muddy dirt road. Roy got out, supposedly yelling for a particular girl. He got out of his car with a baseball bat. He supposedly told the crowd now gathering that if he didn't find this girl, he would beat all of them. As he ran, swinging his bat, the five boys between seventeen and nineteen years old, grabbed bricks and began fighting back.

There was nothing recognizable of Roy's head when they finished. But mother said Carl had performed a miracle and Roy looked like himself. I remembered seeing daddy, who had no battering done to his head, and he didn't look natural. He looked waxy and unlike anyone I knew. I had nightmares for years after his funeral. I had wondered what had happened to my daddy, where had he gone and who was this man in my daddy's casket. I didn't like any of this stuff.

After we went back to Mother's and I politely said hello to the callers, I put my shoes on and told mother I was going for a run. She didn't understand this and felt I should stay and play hostess, but I knew to save my sanity I had to get out of there.

My mother lived in a little subdivision at the edge of town. Two streets over and I was on a county tar road. Just paved enough to move easily. I was not a runner, but from time to time I ran. I loved the springtime in south Georgia. The dogwoods were in bloom, the azaleas were brilliant and all the spring flowers were beginning to come to life. I ran and tried to think what I felt about Roy. Roy's death. Roy's life. My life—with and without Roy. I ran until I panted and my side ached. I wanted to keep running and not stop. There was too much to think about and too many unanswered questions. I wasn't even sure if there were answers.

By the time I got back to the house, my brother Jack had arrived from Chicago. Jack hated to fly; consequently, when he did fly he numbed his fear with a few drinks. He was tipsy, but I was happy to see him. We sat in the back yard under the big oak tree and talked, but not about anything that was in our hearts. Just tidbits of how many drinks he had had, some jokes he'd heard. Not anything about our older brother, how Roy would tell us to look up at the ceiling while he took favorite bites of food off our plates, then exclaim, "It must have been some strange thing that got your food!" He was the "strange thing" but we fell for it every time. Or how he convinced me, on one of my trips home, he had gone into gardening and had won a prize for the largest cucumber grown in Colquitt County. I was so thrilled that he had acquired a healthy habit and I praised him and encouraged him to continue gardening. Hours later when I was leaving I happened to look in the backyard (where all the gardening supposedly took place) and saw weeds almost to the rooftop. Roy saw my look of anger, once again, I let myself be duped, and couldn't stop laughing. Nor did we talk about the time I drove home on paper-thin tires and Roy insisted he drive with me to Tallahassee to get a new set. Nor when I sent my darling Lorri to stay two weeks with my mother while I gave all my attention to my soon-to-be teenager, Melissa. While Lorri was with my mother, Roy would get her and take her to his house. He spent time with her and with Melissa while she was there.

And we didn't come close to talking about Roy threatening to do bodily harm while he was in prison to several people if they didn't let him get to a phone and call me when Lyle's plane went down. I don't know if he was crying when he was talking with me, but he was choked up. He really liked Lyle. Roy didn't like a lot of people.

And we didn't talk about Roy giving me my first drink when his twin boys were born. We had been at the hospital and came back to

Roy's house. He had married Retha, the widow of a car dealership owner, who had a ten-year-old boy. Roy had been working at the dealership six months earlier while Retha's husband was in the hospital in Atlanta. Roy would drive the 400-mile round trip, taking Retha up to visit her husband. Ironically, Retha didn't drive. She was attractive in a quiet, mousy way, and when her husband died, she inherited the dealership. I was eighteen at the time, and I could see the cogs turning in Roy's mind. Roy had been at home, coming off some drug or other. My mother had sent him a bus ticket to get from New Orleans to Moultrie. Later Roy would laughingly tell this story and say, "Not a nickel for coffee. Just enough for a ticket. My mother can take two buffalo nickels, rub them together 'til they shit. That's how good she is at managing money."

My mother was a woman before her time. She kept an eye on Roy twenty-four hours a day for several months while he came off of drugs. Today's rehabilitation centers make a lot of money doing the things she did with Roy in the 1950's. The only problem then, as now, is the person must want to give up the addiction.

Roy began spending all of his time with Retha and showing attention to her ten-year-old boy. Vulnerability on Retha's part, greed on Roy's; a match made in hell. The night they came by the house to tell us they were getting married, I asked Roy not to do it. He had a flask in his back pocket and patting the flask, he said, "It'll be okay."

Retha was as golden as an angel. She glowed she was so happy. I said, "Retha don't do this. You will only get hurt."

She smiled her angelic, glowing smile and said, "Jan, you're only eighteen. You don't know anything about love."

Some months later, Retha had twin boys. I went with Roy and his friend back to Roy's house and he poured us some wine. I didn't drink but felt I should this time to celebrate the birth of the twins, Roy and Ronnie. I drank the wine and as I was leaving Roy was laughing and said, "If the room begins to whirl when you go to bed, put your foot on the floor. That will stop it." All night long I was putting one foot on the floor, changing to the other, but the room didn't stop whirling.

Roy was a contradiction. He was loving and protective one moment and in the blink of an eye, he was murderous. Many years later when we were much older and should have been mature, I was frightened within an inch of my life. Roy pulled a gun on me. I had come to Moultrie to visit my mother. I had been living in Japan for two years. I came back alone, leaving my husband and five children. My mother and Roy picked me up at the airport. I had been flying many hours, was tired, needed a shower and was glad to be out of the airplane. I was surprised to see Roy. I didn't know where he was or how he was since I had been in the Orient. He was living with Mother. We went to her house and as soon as we got in the house my brother said, "How about a drink, Jan? I know you must be tired." I nearly fainted from his concern and his manners.

Drinking had been a big bone of contention all of my life. People in my family didn't know how to drink. At least I thought it was a matter of knowing how much to drink, but most importantly to stay civil when you did drink. No arguing, no fighting, no nasty tempers. Stay sophisticated and be pleasant. Laugh, be witty, have intellectual conversation. I said, "Sure, I would love a drink."

He fixed a Jack Daniels with water and set it in front of me. Mother seldom drank so I was not surprised that she didn't have one. We sat at Mother's kitchen table. I began to relax and had had a couple of sips of my drink when I noticed Roy pouring a large amount of Jack Daniels into his glass. He was talking faster and faster, but I wasn't "into" it. I was just happy to be home and be with my mother. Having my brother there was like an added blessing. Neither of them were asking me about my family or what my life was like or what it was like living in Japan. That wasn't unusual, but I kept hoping things would change. Before I realized it Roy was emptying the remains of Jack Daniels in his glass. He was talking a lot about Daddy and said, "Tomorrow we are going over to Daddy's grave."

"No way," I said. "I am exhausted, it's close to midnight and I don't go to graves." I thought I said it in a pleasant adult way, but now Roy was shouting.

"You never loved Daddy, anyway! That's how you treat your Daddy? Well, he never loved you, either. I'm the only one who ever loved him." Roy was crying, pacing the floor and mumbling.

Mother was trying to calm him down, throwing dirty looks at me. "Calm down, Roy, it's okay. Jan will go, won't you, Jan? Tell Roy you will go in the morning. We'll all go and we'll go by Peggy's. Tell him you'll go."

I was getting agitated that at age thirty-six, I was still being controlled and told what to do even though I had calmly and patiently expressed my wishes. "No, I will not go," I said.

Roy stomped out of the kitchen into the bedroom and immediately was back, standing in the doorway with a gun in his hand, pointed at me. Mother jumped over and grabbed the gun out of Roy's hand. With a cry Roy turned around, walked four feet back to the bedroom, fell across the bed and passed out.

The three weeks I was to stay and visit with my mother turned into three days. That was the soonest I could get a flight out of Moultrie. I stayed in my mother's room for three days, reading, writing, praying I could get home back to Japan and to my husband and children.

I'm sure Jack didn't know about that incident. Years later I tried to talk to mother about it and she said I had made it up. Love and hate, living and dying were all mixed up, I think, for all of us. Maybe more so for Roy.

The first time Roy met my second husband, Lennie, he took Lennie out to Johnny's, the local roadhouse. Most people drove up to Johnny's, sat in the car and ordered a beer or something stronger. Roy and Lennie went inside. There were some "girls of the night" who frequented Johnny's and I suspect Roy frequented them. As Roy and Lennie ordered a beer, Roy asked Lennie which "girl" he wanted. Lennie didn't understand what Roy was asking.

Roy said, "You know, Lennie, which girl do you want to sleep with? Johnny has a room upstairs and you can use that."

Lennie looked at Roy in amazement then started laughing. "Roy, you are something else."

Roy said, "No, Lennie, I am not something else. Which fucking girl do you want to go upstairs and fuck? That's what I'm asking."

Lennie just stared at Roy. Finally he said, "Roy, I can see you are serious. Thanks, but no thanks. Your sister is all the woman I want. She's my dream."

Roy grinned and said, "Good. I would have had to kill you if you had taken me up on the offer."

When Lennie told me this I was horrified. He said he had no doubt Roy meant what he said. Years later, Roy told me the exact same story. He said that his reason was that if Lennie was going to play around on me, he would stop it before it got started. When I told Mother this story later, she laughed and said, "Roy is such a kidder."

On that same trip my brother took my son Paul, age seven, and my stepson, age sixteen, out for a drive around Moultrie. When he asked the boys what they thought would make this depressed town boom, young Paul replied "a bomb." My brother told this story all over town about how smart his nephew was.

Roy could be charming, as when I was graduating from high school and playing in the band. Roy went with Mother and Daddy and said he knew exactly where I was sitting because he could see my foot tapping and he knew that was me. Or when Roy was ten and Mother would boil a wash pot full of peanuts, so Roy could put them in nickel bags and sell them, and he always had customers.

But then there was the time when Mother had her hysterectomy at age sixty-five and I rushed home to be with her. She was awfully afraid of being in the hospital. Working in one gave her no confidence when it came to being a patient. She was in ICU and it felt to me like she would never come out. I was afraid she would die. Finally, she was in her room, all hooked up to IV's, tubes and monitors, sleeping peacefully when Roy came in. I had promised my mother I would not leave her and I didn't. I stayed in her room, slipping into the bathroom to freshen up when she would drift off to sleep. I was sitting by her bed, journaling, when Roy came in. I realized he was drunk when he walked over and grabbed my journal out of my hands. "Now I'll read what you're always scribbling. Writing about me, I'll bet. Saying nasty things, I'm sure."

By this point he was yelling. I tried getting my journal and he rushed around the end of the bed, getting out of my way. As he came on the other side of the bed he lost his footing and fell across mother's stomach, pulling out one of the IV's. I was crying, yelling at him to get out. He said, "No. I'm going to beat the shit out of you."

I ran out of the room, he was running behind me, but stumbling, and I was able to reach the corridor to the next wing. There was a broom closet and I jumped in there and closed the door. I could hear him calling me. For what seemed like hours I huddled in that little room, scared to death for my own safety, but worried about my mother and what Roy might do to her.

Finally, I chanced opening the door. I looked up and down the halls and not seeing or hearing anyone I came out. I found a doctor, told him the situation, crying my eyes out from shame, fear and worry about my mother's health. The doctor made it clear he would have Roy locked up quicker than a New York minute.

Again, when I relayed this incident to my mother and my anger, shame and humiliation at his behavior in the hospital where she worked, she just told me I was too sensitive. Somehow it came out as my fault.

Jack and I did not discuss any of these things when he came down for Roy's funeral. We sat up late, Jack drinking, me wanting to connect to any member of my family, but unable to do so.

The next morning I helped Mother do some things, then went to the store to pick up some panty hose. When I returned, Mother and Jack were sitting at the kitchen table. Jack was shaking his head back and forth and before I could get inside my mother said, "I can't believe you could be so stupid."

There was that word. For as long as I could remember I was told I was "dumb, stupid and ugly." What had I done now, I wondered?

Jack was muttering under his breath, but loud enough for me to hear "dumb, dumb, dumb."

"How can you do something so dumb?" Mother asked.

"If you will tell me what I did, maybe I can help clarify the situation," I said, trying to stay calm, while my heart was racing.

"Well, you'll just have to pay, I'm sure—and big bucks I'll bet. And stop being the professor and using such fancy words." All of this came from Jack and I still didn't have a clue what they were talking about.

"Can you just tell me what's happened?" I asked.

"Lorri wrecked your car, you dumb, stupid little girl." There it was. Jack worked in most of the label.

"What?" I was screaming. "How do you know? What happened? Where is she? Is she okay?" I was babbling, close to tears. My baby. My child. Was she okay?

"She called just a while ago and said she had a concussion, but she was okay. Sherry or somebody like that took her to the hospital."

I ran to my mother's bedroom to call Lorri. She answered and we were both crying. She had taken the car the night before to go to play practice and a car had hit her. Not much damage to the car and, no, she didn't have a concussion but was scared.

Once I knew she was okay I lectured. But what I was really doing was lashing out at her because I was impotent with my mother and brother. I could talk and explain 'til I was blue in the face, and they would not, could not hear me. I grounded Lorri and hung up the phone.

My brother was dead, my other brother was staying as close to inebriated without going totally over the edge, and my mother was tongue lashing everyone she could reach. But still it seemed I was the favorite target.

We buried Roy. His twin sons Roy and Ronnie came and were torn apart. My heart went out to them. From what I had heard through the years, they had had a volatile, on again off again, irritable relationship with their father. Here was more unfinished business with the dead.

I left the next day to return to work. I had missed one day, Friday, and would be back on Monday morning. My boss, Mr. "Furious" had called and Lorri told him my brother had died. I had told her not to tell anyone he was murdered. I was too ashamed. He told Lorri I should have come to work anyway. He was very rude to her and with all that was going on, she was crushed.

I had not slept for days, and not at all while I was at Mother's, so my emotions were raw. No tears of sadness, no good-bye to my brother Roy. Only pent up emotions. Chewing out from my mother, Jack on the sidelines chanting, "Dumb, dumb, dumb." When I arrived at the Dallas/Fort Worth Airport, Paul, my son, was suppose to meet me, but I couldn't find him. I sat down in the waiting area. I didn't know what I felt and not knowing how to explore my feelings, I just went numb, then became angry. Anger was the only emotion I could identify and since I didn't know how to handle that I got depressed. When Paul walked up, for the first time since being told Roy was murdered, I burst into tears. Paul hugged me and took me home.

When I first got home Lorri was contrite but soon became belligerent and combative. Before I realized what I was doing I slapped her in the face, the side where her braces were. She screamed and ran to her room. I sank into the sofa and wanted to die. If I could do something to take that slap back I would have. Lorri was my sweet, loving child. I had never hit her, never had to scold her much. She was such an easy child to be with and the last thing I wanted was to hurt her. So my whole life was in an uproar, and I didn't know what to do or how to fix it. Things would not get better for a while.

I was at my desk Monday morning before 7:30 A.M. Most of the staff at the Dallas Adult Probation Department didn't arrive 'til closer to 8:00 A.M. "Mr. Furious," my boss, was early, but I usually got in before he did. Still trying to prove what a good girl I was.

My clients started coming in to make their reports to me. As is the case in most cities, my clientele was mostly young black males. The same description as the young men who had killed my brother. What kind of reaction would I have when a nineteen-year-old black man on probation for murder came in to report to me, I wondered?

Around 10:00 A.M. "Mr. Furious" came into my office and said, "Why didn't you bring the sandwiches?"

I said, "Sir, Lorri told you my brother died. I went home to Georgia for his funeral."

"That's no excuse. You were supposed to bring sandwiches, home made, none of that catering stuff you want to do, but homemade! And you didn't do it!" His veins were bunched up in his neck; his face was turning red.

We had all been subjected to Furious's wrath and it was not a pretty sight. Having grown up in a household of yelling, shouting and doors slamming, I always felt breathless and fearful around anyone who did this.

But not this time. All the pent up anger, pain, loss, isolation, and lack of support erupted and spilled all over my office. I was yelling. "How dare you talk about sandwiches when my brother just died? And my daughter had a wreck and a near concussion and you don't say 'How are you, Jan?' or 'Can I do anything Jan?' or anything that would say you are human. Get out of my office—NOW!" I was standing and pointing to the door. Some of the other staff were peeking around their doors to see what on earth was going on. They had never heard me raise my voice and certainly not to my boss!

He left. I was shaking, close to tears, but called in my next client and put on my professional face and went back to business. I wasn't aware that I had three days of family leave after a death coming to me. The next morning I called-in and arranged to take my three days, plus a week's vacation leave. 'Let them fire me,' I thought, just one more failure in my life.

10

Pat

At times I felt so alone because I did not have anyone to turn to. I felt like God was out to lunch, or at least He wasn't answering the phone. I didn't feel connected. I felt lost, but even within the depths of my despair, inside my soul, I knew that God was still there, even if I wasn't connected to him. As I searched my inner being, I began to realize that fear was the root cause for that disconnection. What if I could turn that "f" word, fear, back into faith? If I could I'd know that God would be there for me. I already knew in my heart, in the big picture that, God was there with me; that God was there for me; and that He was real.

No one knows what demons dwell in the depths of our deception. For thirteen years after the death of Lennie I was alone. I had received degrees from college, which was one of the goals I had set for myself when I graduated from high school. When I graduated from high school at sixteen, I had four goals:

1) get a degree from college

2) fly with the airlines as a stewardess

3) be a model

4) be married to the same man for 50 years.

Obviously, my fourth goal was not going to happen. That realization came to me after Lennie's death. I was thirty-six-years old when Lennie died, which was ten years after Lyle was killed. But I had flown with the airlines and I had modeled and when I turned forty I entered college.

When I graduated from high school, my high school senior year English teacher had gotten a scholarship for me to go to Mercer University, but Daddy said, "No, you cannot go." However, later on, Daddy asked me if I would like to go to Fort Worth Texas, to the Southwestern Baptist Theological Seminary. I said, "Yes, I would love to go."

I would have been happy to go anywhere, just to go to college . Texas was not even in my realm of thinking because it was so far away. I had never been anywhere except for Georgia and Florida. I was about to turn seventeen when Daddy told me that I had to be eighteen to attend the Seminary. He offered to go to Jacksonville, Florida, to see his friend who was on the board of directors of the seminary. He would try to see if he could get me a waiver to attend a year early. Daddy followed through, saw his friend, came back from Jacksonville, and told me that he had obtained a waiver and that I could attend the seminary in Fort Worth after I turned seventeen. He told me that he and my mother would drive me out to Ft. Worth. My mother started packing my things in preparation for the trip. She sewed new clothes and got my new wardrobe together. Suddenly, about two or three weeks later, just about when it was time for us to go, my father came in and said, "Jan, no, you cannot go." I was devastated. I had so wanted to go to college. Ironically, 52 years later my son received his master's degree from the Southwestern Baptist Theological Seminary in Fort Worth, Texas.

I received my college degree in my forties and I became a probation officer. I worked for the Dallas County adult probation for three years.

Frequently on weekends, I would go up to Lake Tacoma to visit my dear friend Dee. While I was there, we would visit one of the club and have drinks and dinner and Dee and I would talk. Usually there would be a few guys around who would come over. They'd ask us to dance and some of them seemed interested in me, but I was there to have fun and did not have any particular interest in any of them.

On one particular weekend, March 5th, 1982, I went to visit Dee for the weekend. She said, "Come on, there is someone who I want you to meet." I considered that it was just one friend meeting another friend. She introduced me to Pat.

Pat told me that the minute he looked into my eyes he knew that he was home. We talked that night but for me there was nothing earth shattering, nothing that said to me this was love at first sight. I just thought that he was very nice.

I had some engine trouble and had to leave my car there. I went back the following weekend to get it and I saw Pat again at the same club. He walked up and leaned over the table and said, "Who is your favorite author?" I just about fell over because I had never met anyone who had approached me in that manner. The great seduction happened right then because he appealed to my mind. We started talking about books and reading, and I found him thoroughly fascinating. This pattern continued. I would go up on weekends and we would see each other and talk. Pat was in the middle of a divorce, but I didn't think that anything would come of our relationship. I had pretty much given up on ever finding love or being in love again. I did not think that that was going to be part of my life.

We continued to cross paths on weekends. Then one weekend, there was an emergency in my family, and Pat just showed up. He was there to support me and said, "Jan, don't even consider that I'm here, just pretend I'm not around. I just want you to know that I am here if you need me, but I don't want you to spend time worrying about me or my particular comfort now." His consideration completely blew me away.

Then he asked me to marry him. I was very surprised, and I did not know what I was going to do. Six months later we were married. We both loved to party and have drinks and visit with friends. We had a good time together not only because he was someone whom I loved, but we were good friends.

Pat had a great sense of humor. He had a kind and funny way of putting me at ease. One time we were talking about my life, how one husband had died of a heart attack and another in a plane crash.

He said, "Don't you worry, Jan, I'm not going anywhere. However, if a lady comes along with a handicap sticker on her car and chocolate cake in her hand, then I'm out of here." We laughed at his joke.

Pat was passionate about everything in life. He loved good food, he loved good talk and I'm happy to say he loved me. Pat and I had a great life together. We loved going to the Gulf Coast and spending time on the beach. Pat would get off from work, come home, we'd change into our bathing suits, then go and relax by the pool; just enjoying each other's company. I remember when he came home from work one time; we were in the bedroom changing clothes, then he stopped and put arms around me and said, "What more could any man want?" As he said that I just shrieked and ran from the room. I just stood in the other room shaking.

Pat came in and said, "Jan, what on earth is the matter? What has happened?"

I told Pat what Lyle had said to me. And what Lennie had said to me, the same identical words.

He held me and hugged me and said, "No wonder why my words shook you." He said again "Don't worry Jan, I am not going to leave you." I suddenly had such cold chills from hearing again, "What more could any man want?" It had never occurred to me before then that Pat and I would not live together into old, old age.

About a year and a half after Pat and I were married, a family member of mine went into rehab for substance abuse. I went as a family member because as I learned although I did not know then at the time, that alcoholism is a family disease. I went and spent one week with my loved one and was amazed because I had never been in an environment like that before. I had never been in a rehabilitation center. It was a place of total acceptance, of total love, a place where you were accepted for who you were and not judged. It was who you were, what you were about and not how much money you made or your social status. It was about the person. I was so taken in by that environment. When I came back after a week, I was miserable every time I had even just a glass of champagne. Although I

122

only had an occasional drink, a glass of champagne, or a beer with Pat, I was miserable because I had learned so much about what alcohol, even a small amount, can do to a person's brain cells. Having grown up where I was told I was dumb, stupid and ugly I was cognizant of the fact that maybe I wasn't so smart. As a result, I did not want to be burning up the brain cells that I did have. And so I began to question those drinks that Pat and I were having at night.

On July 4th, we went to his office party. There was a keg of beer there and we had a few beers and then went home. Later that evening we sat on the patio and talked. I told Pat about what I had learned at the rehab center, about how alcohol kills off brain cells. Pat said to me the next morning that it was like sitting out on the patio with Carrie Nation. His evening was not very festive with me lecturing. But I began to pay attention to what I was drinking and became miserable when I thought about it. Here I was, I had a beautiful home, lovely things, and had a husband who I was crazy about. Everything on paper looked great, but on the inside I was not happy; I was just miserable.

We had a condo in Florida, so we took a couple of weeks vacation and went down there. While we were there, we did a good bit of drinking. On the way home I told Pat, "this has to stop, all this drinking is just way too much." Although we weren't hurting anyone or doing anything bad to anyone, inside I was still miserable.

When we returned to Dallas I called the rehab center. I told them that I wanted to come there and stay for a month. So I made arrangements to go and when I told Pat about it, he was not happy at all. He said, "You don't have a problem, this is ridiculous."

I said, "This is what I have to do. I do it with your support, or I do it alone, but I have to do this."

When I went to the rehab center, I did not know if I was going to have a marriage when I came back. Pat loved to drink as much as I did. We loved to have a good time and we loved to party. And here I was about to throw a wrench into the whole scenario. Still, I went. I spent an entire month and I cried. I cried the whole time that I was there. What I learned while I was there was even though I talked about my life, or some things that had happened to me, I never went for the solution. I did not know there was a solution. I did not even know how to form that concept. When I went to the rehab center, I was so out of touch with my feelings, I did not even know how to describe how I felt. I did not even know what I felt. The counselor would hold up a list of feelings and say to me just point, do you feel this do you feel that?

So little by little I began to identify my feelings. And I realized that I had never actually grieved. I had never grieved over any of the deaths in my life, or the trauma I experienced from the time I was six-years-old. I had never grieved, I just stuffed all of my feelings deep down inside of me. What I learned in rehab is that any chemical, including alcohol, that is ingested only covers or blocks your true feelings. Then deaden your feelings. So I spent a month at the rehab center and learned to cry. That for me was the pinnacle of what the work was about, gaining the ability to cry. I learned how to let my feelings come to the surface and just let them be. That was very hard for me because, for all these years, especially as a military wife, I had been given great praise for how stoic I was. For example, when I didn't show any emotion at Lennie's service and the missing man formation that flew overhead.

After about a year of being in AA, Pat developed a heavy, raspy cough. I asked Pat to go to the doctor, but he resisted. Finally, I appealed to him by saying, "I love you with all my heart and soul. I want to spend the rest of my life with you. But I refuse to continue living like this with you and not knowing what is wrong with you."

He went to Dr. and they diagnosed him with bronchitis and gave him medication. Still he continued to cough. Finally, after two weeks he went back to the doctor. This time, the diagnosis was lung cancer. Just before his diagnosis, Chip Moody, who was a local broadcaster, wrote an article for the paper talking about his diagnosis with Hotchkins Disease; it was a very touching article. It talked about the first indication of the problem was a cough he had developed. I asked Pat if he had read the article.

Pat snapped back, "Yes, I read the article, and I do not want to talk about it." That was typical of the way Pat dealt with things that bothered him.

For example, once we were watching a documentary about Vietnam veterans. As the soldiers talked about their experiences, I began to cry. When the program was over I composed myself and turned to Pat and asked, "Honey you served two tours in Vietnam, talk to me about that time, about your experience and what you went through." He just looked at me and his eyes got very cold. I had never seen him look this way before. He said, "I will go to my grave before I talk about anything having to do with Vietnam and what went on there." That was pretty much the way that he was.

He was a very funny man, and he made me laugh, which was one of the things I loved so much about him. But still, he had a lot of pain and a lot of hurt inside of him. And as he told me he would, he went to his grave, without telling me or anyone about his time in Vietnam.

He was diagnosed in December of 1986. He began chemotherapy shortly thereafter. He wrote to me in March after his third session of chemotherapy. He left the letter in the kitchen with instructions for me not to open it until he was gone to the hospital to continue his chemotherapy.

Of course, the minute he cleared the back door I grabbed the letter and opened it. What he said was, *the chemotherapy is not working and I know that I am dying*. This news was so upsetting that it made me completely crazy. If it were not for AA, going there, crying and letting my emotions out I firmly believe to this day that I would not be alive.

I don't know that I would have consciously committed suicide, but I am sure that in an attempt to smother my grief, I would have taken sleeping pills and alcohol. I would have turned to those chemicals that got me by before and I would not have made it. But with the support of people in AA and working the program, I was able to manage.

As Pat had told me, the chemotherapy was not working so, the doctors started radiation treatments. Pat would leave the house and go to the VA hospital, get radiation treatments, then go to his office. He worked all day and came home. I do not know how he kept up that pace. The few times I went with him to the hospital, I was completely wiped out. For weeks he maintained this schedule.

Three weeks before he died the doctor said that he three choices. "You can quit work, go into the hospital or get yourself another doctor." Pat quit work and came home. I could tell that he was getting worse. I had originally thought that we had another year and a half together and that with treatment and miracles he would maybe live even longer. I was journaling at that time and I wrote in my journal, that *I wish this were over.* I don't know if Pat read my journal, but I think he did because he said to me one night when that he was very upset and frustrated over his condition, "I bet you wish I was just dead."

I said, "No, not at all, I want for you to be well. I want this situation to be over so that we can be back to where we were."

A couple of times his sadness and frustration got the better of him. This would cause him to yell at me. During these times I would sit next to him on the bed and tell him, "I love you, I will be here for you always, but you can never talk to me like this again. If you do, I'm leaving." He never talked to me that way again.

I tried to get him to talk to me about dying and what his wishes were. But he could not do it, we could just not *go there.* He did tell me that the previous Christmas when he was diagnosed, that he went to North Park Mall and sat on a bench by the reflecting pool. At that moment he looked up and saw Lorri walking towards him. He said at that point he realized that he would never be in this spot again at North Park Mall and he would never see Lorri again; this would be his last Christmas.

I knew from what he said that he understood he was not going to be with us much longer. The Sunday before I took him to the hospital, Missi was there. I had gone out for only a few minutes, but when I returned to the house Missi was there, and she came out and said to me, "I am really freaked-out."

"What's wrong?" I asked

She said, "I did not know where Pat was and when I called out he said that he was in the bedroom and for me to go in. When I got in there he was sitting on the side of the bed and told me to sit down. I sat down next him and he said to me, 'Honey this will all be over in another week.' He did not say anymore, but I just freaked-out."

"He is just upset," I said.

She said, "I think you need to listen to him because he knows more than we do about his body."

On Monday he had swollen up so badly that his legs were twice the size they normally were, and he had stopped eating. I told him that he had to go to the hospital that he could not continue as he was. He finally consented to go. Missi and I took him out to the hospital and got him checked in. It was 5:00 P.M. by the time we finished the paperwork and got him checked into his room. Concerned for how we were feeling, Pat insisted that Missi and I go to an AA meeting. I did not want to leave him, I wanted to stay there with him. But he insisted that we leave and go to an AA meeting. We did what he asked.

The next morning I was back at the hospital, and I stayed with him as the doctors came in and out several times. There was one doctor who I had gotten close with and talked to several times. He was a jazz musician and was also working on his residency. He hugged me and said, "Pat is not going to last much longer."

I was in the room later that afternoon when Pat's son came by. Pat told his son what a wonderful son he had been and how proud he was of him. After Pat's son left, I sat next to him on the bed. He told me that he felt far away and wanted to go home. I tried to explain to him that he could not, that there was no way that I could take care of him at home. He said, "No, you don't understand I want to go home." Then he said to me, "Do you know how much I love you?"

I said, "Yes. And do you know how much I love you?"

And he said, "Tell me."

I said, "I love you enough to let you go. I will let you go to the light."

He just looked into the far distance and he said, "I want to rest now." I walked over to the sink to wash my hands, and I noticed that they were out of paper towels, so I walked into the vacant room next door, and when I got back into the hall I heard "Jan." I rushed into his room. I put my arms round his neck. I lifted his head a little bit off the pillow. He said, "Jan," and then sighed. He died there in my arms. I held him and kissed him. Then the nurses and the doctor came rushing in. They pulled me away from Pat. There were two other patients in with him, one of them got up and put his arms around me and asked, "What happened in here earlier? I've never felt anything like that before."

And he was right. There was a presence in the room that was all encompassing. I said, "It was God."

He said, "I never felt that before. I do believe that God was in the room with us."

The nurse told me that I would have to leave the room and wanted to know if there was anyone there with me. I said "No." She said, "You cannot stay in the room. You have to go to the reception area on the third floor." I called Lorri from there.

There were other people in the reception area. I sat down but I did not cry. I thought to myself, 'This is so strange. This is unbelievable, my husband just died. What am I going to do? I don't know what I feel, I don't know what's going on.' Then one of the people in the reception area noticed I was in a daze. She asked me, "Are you all right?"

I told her, "My husband just died and I don't know what I feel and I don't know what is going on."

She wanted to know what she could do to help. I teared up and told them that my daughter was coming. I just sat there and waited.

I prepared a memorial service for Pat. He wanted to be cremated with his ashes scattered in the Gulf of Mexico. After the memorial service his daughter came up to me and said, "I want to thank you for giving my dad the happiest five years of his life. And thank you for changing him."

I said, "I didn't change him. All I did was allow him to be who he truly was."

She said, "I have never seen him like that before. You two were so happy together."

I took Pat's ashes to the Gulf and scattered them in the ocean where he wanted to be. A week after Pat died, I came home one day at dusk. I walked in and realized how lonely the house was. I felt sad and dejected. I sat down in the living room, put my head back against the chair, closed my eyes and just reflected on my life. I wondered what I was going to do now that I was widowed again.

Out of the corner of my eye, over on the sofa, I thought, what is happening? Am I losing my mind? I thought that I was going crazy. Sitting on the sofa was Lyle and Pat and Lennie. I started to jump-up and scream or whatever and they said, "It's okay. We're here. We just want you to know that we're here, we love you, we're watching over you."

All three of them were smiling, they said, "We're happy, we are at peace and we want you to be at peace. We want you to be happy. And we want you to know that we are always looking over you, watching over you." I just sat there, as peace washed over me with the feeling of pure love; it was an incredible experience. I didn't tell anyone about it for years for fear that they would lock me up some place.

All three of them were there and they have come to me many times since. They have told me that they are watching over me, they loved me and they are here for me.

I know that meeting and marrying Pat was Divinely Ordained. After Lennie, I didn't think that I would ever marry again. Meeting Pat and falling in love with him and marrying him brought all the other deaths around me into view and helped me to understand, no, I have never understood, but to help me accept their deaths and to know that love goes on and that I could and can love. It opened me up to accept and receive love. And I think had I not met Pat and married him, that I probably would have been bitter; certainly an incomplete woman. He just seemed to bring things around full circle. He was also a great influence on my children's lives. They all adored him as he did them.

In reflecting back now on my seventy years, I think that the one thing I have learned, which is the most important thing, is love. I think the next most important thing is forgiveness. I have learned to accept and forgive my parents. I have learned and accepted and forgiven the deaths. I have forgiven myself for my mistakes, for my lack of knowledge. I think that if we can learn to mature into our own responsibilities, our own actions and not blame them on other people that is when we learn true love and that is when we become a complete human being. I think forgiveness is the core of that.

Epilogue

I hope that my story has not been too depressing. Having dealt with depression off and on throughout most of my life until the last few years, I understand what *that is* about.

What I wanted to do in telling you my story is to convey that there is hope. All I can offer you is my experience, strength and hope and to know that no matter how dark the clouds and how bad things get, if you have hope and faith, you can hang on, you can get through.

This is just the tip of the iceberg of my story; I haven't told my entire story. That would take volumes. But by telling you some of the experiences I have had and where I am today, you will know that I am so content and so joyous. The reason is because I have faith. I know that there is going to be a better tomorrow and I know that whatever is going on and whatever is happening, no matter how bad it is, that it is going to get better. As long as I can hang on to my faith and not get into the fear, then I know that I will survive; that I will be okay. Not just okay, not just survive, but to thrive. I learn from what life hands me and that helps me to be a better person.

I live my life in joy and faith. I travel, I have great friends, my family is wonderful. Life is good. God is good.

Books available through

Living Legacy Press
www.living.legacy-press.com

Order Form

Living Legacy Press
603 Louis Henna Boulevard, S B-170 #122
Round Rock, Texas 7864 • 512-907-1821

Mail Check or Money Order to:
Jan Guest

Name _____ Date _____

Address _____

City _____ State _____ Zip Code _____

Day telephone _____

Evening telephone

Book title _____

Number of books ordered: _____ X $12.95   Total cost $ _____

Shipping and handling $4.50 per book $ _____

Total amount due $ _____

___ check   ___ money order   ___ VISA   ___ MasterCard

Credit Card number: _____ Exp. date _____

Driver's license number: _____

Signature _____ Date _____